SCIENCE vs CRIME

The Evolution of the Police Lab

Other Books by Eugene B. Block

The Wizard of Berkeley
Great Train Robberies of the West
Great Stagecoach Robberies of the West
The Vindicators
Above the Civil War
And May God Have Mercy
Fifteen Clues
Fabric of Guilt
Famous Detectives
Fingerprinting
The Immortal San Franciscans
Voiceprinting
Hypnosis in Criminal Investigation
Lie Detectors

SCIENCE vs CRIME

The Evolution of the Police Lab

EUGENE B. BLOCK

cp

cragmont publications

SCIENCE vs. CRIME
Copyright © 1979 by Eugene B. Block

Published by
Cragmont Publications
China Basin Building
161 Berry Street, Suite 6410
San Francisco, California 94107

Distributed to the book trade by
Caroline House
P.O. Box 161
Thornwood, New York 10594

Edited by Diane Sipes
Jacket designed by Carolyn Bean Associates
Type set by Medallion Graphics
Printed by Science Press
Bound by Arnold's Bindery

Manufactured in the United States of America
First printing October, 1979

Library of Congress Cataloging in Publication Data

Block, Eugene B.
      Science vs. crime.

      Includes index.
      1. Criminal investigation.   I. Title.
HV8073.B58   364.12   79-21941
ISBN 0-89666-007-9

To Ruth,
with love

Contents

Acknowledgments

Long, intensive research and much other work required for the writing of this book could not have been accomplished without the valuable and friendly help of scores of men and women throughout the United States and abroad. Unfortunately, it is impossible to name them all here and to extend my individual thanks, but I hope that they will accept my well meant words of gratitude.

Especial thanks are due to my publisher's editorial director Fred E. Felder, publicist Pauline McGuire, and editor Diane Sipes, whose skillful editing of the manuscript added materially to its improvement.

Thanks are due also to Robert Cooper, Tony Sprague, and Pat Zajac of the Alameda County, California Sheriff's Department Crime Lab; to A. Keith Smith, chief of the California State Criminalistics Laboratory; to my beloved wife Ruth W., and to my three sons and their wives — George S. and Alice B. Block, Edwin J. and Marjorie P. Block, and Charles W. and Nancy Block, whose encouragement and help aided in various ways.

Eugene B. Block
San Francisco, California
October, 1979

Foreword

Having spent the greater part of my adult life (33 years) in the field of law enforcement, I am keenly interested in the history of the development of scientific crime detection.

Professional, scientifically obtained evidence for court presentation is more vital than ever in coping successfully with the viciousness and complexity of crimes today.

I am delighted to see that the dedicated and scholarly Eugene B. Block has authored another book in which he has delved into this fascinating subject. The ordinary citizen will find it most interesting, and the professional crime buster will benefit from the factual information clearly set forth.

Thomas H. Cahill
Chief of Police, Retired
San Francisco, California
Past president and life member
of International Association of
Chiefs of Police

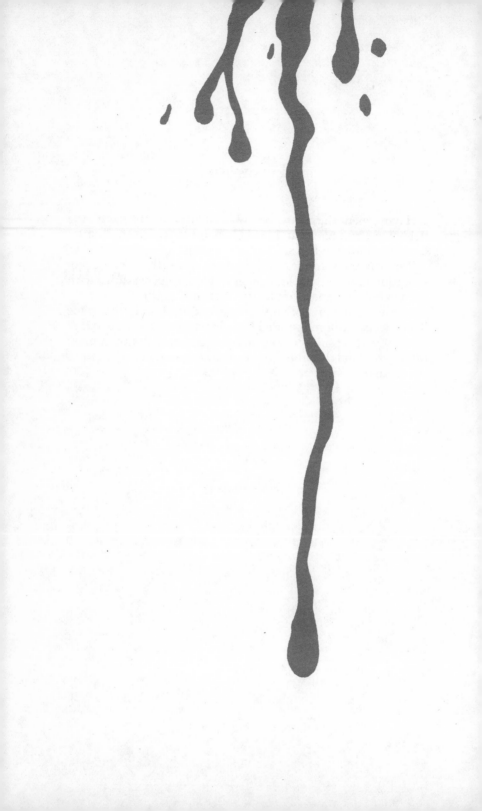

Chapter 1

The Beginning

A SINGLE HAIR, caught in the bristles of a well-worn brush, once solved the mysterious disappearance of a French court attaché and sent his murderer to the guillotine.

A tiny scrap of metal, smaller than a dime, recovered from the wreckage of a passenger plane after a disaster that killed forty-four people, led to the conviction of the man who had secreted a bomb in the airliner and to his death in the gas chamber.

These astonishing scientific accomplishments, performed by skilled criminalists in crime laboratories, epitomized the advances in scientific crime detection that have taken place in the relentless ongoing war of science versus crime. They, and many hundreds like them, illustrate what is being done to make such substances as hair, wood, dirt, blood, and glass speak accusing words against the guilty or open prison doors for the innocent.

These achievements are the work of criminalists — often confused with criminologists, whose field is quite different and far broader. Criminalists generally confine themselves to interpreting and evaluating evidence, the essence of scientific crime detection. The criminologist's interests are wider, including such subjects as penology, the causes of crime, sociological problems, and prison reform.

But before the advent of the criminalist and the crime laboratory, the methods of determining guilt and innocence were extremely unsophisticated, and often bordered on superstition. Yet the work of these early researchers is of importance, since it opened the doors to later concepts of criminal justice and the subsequent application of scientific methods that utilize the natural sciences in interpreting the significance of debris found at the scenes of crimes.

The credit for intensive research into the earliest methods of criminal investigation belongs to Robert Heindl, a distinguished German criminologist born in Munich in 1883. During his long and busy life, he devoted himself to an investigation of the earliest criminal procedures and to the evolution of scientific methods of solving crimes.

Until death halted Heindl's absorbing research in 1958, he made many valuable contributions, including his role in creating Interpol, the international police bureau in Saint-Cloud, France, which exchanges vital information among the police forces of many countries.

Essentially Heindl started out wanting to know where beginnings and advances had been made and by whom. With infinite patience, he uncovered the first known forms of investigative procedures far back in the Dark Ages, when men first came to understand that the identification of offenders was the major requisite to the safeguarding of life and property. The introduction of science did not come until many years later, and then only in very elementary ways.

Heindl learned that a crude system for recording descriptions of wanted criminals and former offenders existed in Egypt under the Ptolemys beginning in about 300 B.C. and also in the Roman Empire. It was a method surprisingly similar to the *portrait parlant* of today, which provides a verbal picture of an individual based on the parts of the body that cannot be altered or disguised. The words literally translated mean a picture drawn from a description of the person involved. After an intensive study of these descriptions, Heindl concluded that they had come into use centuries before the Christian era and that more complicated procedures had been gradually simplified.

Much earlier, many years before Christ, Hammurabi, the sixth king under the Amorite dynasty of Babylon, laid the first foundations for legal trials. In 500 B.C. Athens initiated a system for the examination of facts (evidence) in determining the guilt or innocence of the accused.

Progress continued, and finally a penal code containing exact instructions on evidence was issued by a bishop in Hamburg. Twenty-five years later the Caroline Code of the German states added provisions for the examination of the accused. These advancements, while they were largely in the nature of legal proceedings, obviously depended on intensive and well-planned investigations by the law-enforcing authorities.

Western Europe, strangely, was backward compared with other societies. Notably in England, France and Germany, trial by ordeal began in the tenth century A.D. and continued for many years. This was even followed in the sixteenth century by a system of trial by battle in both civil and criminal matters — a procedure in which issues were determined by mortal combat.

Trial by ordeal resorted to the supernatural and invoked "divine intercession" to settle questions now determined by judges and juries. This was a backward step in the history of crime detection, for little if any investigation preceded the trial by ordeal. Suspicions alone were sufficient to warrant this method of investigation and judgment.

Various cruel and tortuous procedures were prescribed. In the one most frequently used, the unfortunate would be ordered to grasp a metal rod, white with heat, by the right hand and carry it a distance of nine feet before it could be dropped. This done, the seared hand would be carefully bandaged, the dressings to remain unchanged for three days and nights. They then would be removed and the wound subjected to public gaze. If it had healed, the accused would be declared innocent; if not, guilt was considered to have been established, and punishment would be meted out according to the nature and gravity of the offense.

Penalties were gruesome, serving the dual purpose of punishing and identifying the offender for the remainder of his or her life. Death was decreed not only to set an example but to rid the tribe of an evil member who might contaminate the others, just as a rotten apple might ruin a box of good ones. The hand of a convicted thief might be cut off or a slanderer might lose his tongue. Although the Catholic Church, in England and in France, cried out vigorously against trial by ordeal, it was not officially prohibited in England until 1219, by Henry III. Years later, similar action was taken in France.

The struggle to end trial by battle continued in England for almost two centuries. A bill for its abolition was defeated in Parliament in 1640, but the practice was not finally outlawed until 1819.

In the place of these cruel and barbaric methods for determining guilt or innocence, a new system was created, known as trial by confurgation, which began in about 1234 in England. Those accused of crime were now privileged to face a jury of their peers, which was not to hear factual evidence as this is practiced now but rather to learn from friends of the defendant facts pertaining mainly to the character of the accused and whether he or she was capable of committing the offense charged. On this basis alone was judgment rendered. Jury trials based on physical and verbal evidence were to come still later.

Since the identification of offenders was regarded as essential to the protection of an individual's rights as well as those of society, early governments looked for a simple means of putting a lasting mark of guilt on those who had run afoul of the law. The answer was branding, which also served as a means of punishment.

This procedure was started by the Greeks and Romans and continued for many years in Anglo-Saxon countries. A red-hot iron would be pressed against the cheek, though sometimes the hands or other parts of the body suffered similar treatment. In England, gypsies and vagabonds were branded on the breast with a large letter "V."

Surprisingly, this practice lingered long in many countries. In Russia, where those receiving life sentences were branded on the forehead and both cheeks before being sent to Siberia, the penalty was not abolished until 1854, and China persisted in its use until 1905.

England had her own ideas about branding. When clergy were privileged to arrest judgment in criminal cases, those receiving such clemency were branded on the left thumb. No person could be favored more than once. King William III decreed that the cheek should be substituted for the finger under his rule of grace, but not until the reign of Queen Anne, beginning in 1702, was this brutal practice banned for all time.

As time moved on, the administration of criminal justice made gradual progress and more effective methods for the apprehension of law violators evolved.

Yet for too many years, actually until the scientific procedures in criminal investigation had passed the purely experimental stage, investigators depended solely on three strategies — plain everyday plodding, deduction that relied on the intelligence of individual police officers, and help from informers;

the latter resource is still used to a considerable degree today.

In those early years, many innocents suffered from fallacious reasoning or surmises, but officers of the law had no other courses to follow. They pursued in a rather rudimentary way what today is regarded as the gathering of circumstantial evidence.

Interestingly, deduction became the dominant theme of much early fiction, one story dating as far back as two centuries before the Christian era. Another popular work came many years later, from the pen of Voltaire, who died in 1778. Whether such works of fiction were inspired by the commonly known methods of the police or whether the imaginative plots had a suggestive influence on investigators is a moot point. Probably it was something of an interplay of both.

The first known imaginative writing based on deductive reasoning is found in the Apocrypha of the Old Testament. Translated from the Greek and Latin in 1611 A.D. and believed to have been written during the last two centuries before the Christian era, it is known as the Story of Susanna and has been called by authorities one of the finest short stories in world literature. In some biblical texts, it has been added to the Book of Daniel.

According to the story, Susanna, the wife of Joakin of Babylon, had by her unusual beauty and grace, unknowingly aroused the passionate desires of two elders, men with the power and authority of judges. On a day when the two could no longer restrain their passions, they hid in Susanna's garden until she arrived prepared to bathe. Suddenly they appeared before her, boldly asserting their evil demands but with the threat that if she did not accede they would testify that they had seen her in the arms of a younger man.

Susanna refused. She was publicly accused of adultery, and sentenced to death — a penalty that would have been imposed but for the intervention of Daniel, who cunningly resorted to deduction to prove her innocence. Summoning the two perjurers before an agitated crowd, Daniel publicly interrogated the pair separately so that neither could hear the responses of the other. The first elder, asked where Susanna had been seen with her alleged "lover," promptly replied, "Under the mastic tree." But when his colleague insisted that he had seen them "under the evergreen oak," Daniel quickly deduced that both men were lying. Susanna was promptly vindicated.

Voltaire's work on the same deductive theme, written centuries later, is entitled *The Dog and the Horse*, though it is more popularly known as "The Story of Zadig." Like the earlier tale, it is laid in Babylon.

The story tells of Zadig, who was rambling through the woods when he encountered one of the queen's eunuchs, who inquired anxiously whether he had seen a missing dog on a horse. Shaking his head, Zadig asked if the other was referring to a bitch, slightly lame with long ears, and a horse with small hoofs, about five feet tall and a tail three and a half feet long. The eunuch replied with a question, "Then you've seen them both?" he asked eagerly. Again Zadig insisted that he had not.

The conclusion was that Zadig had stolen both animals. He was arrested, found guilty, and sentenced to life imprisonment, but when the missing animals were found soon afterward the sentence was reduced to a heavy fine.

Zadig, however, continued to insist that he was innocent. He told the queen's men that while he had actually never seen the two animals, he had described them by simple deduction from close and keen observation. The dog's sex, he said, he had determined by droppings on the ground and its lameness by footprints; the horse's size had been surmised by measuring the height of the dust rubbed off on trees along the roadway. The other details had come by similar reasoning.

The king's court was so greatly impressed by Zadig's deductive powers that he was promptly vindicated and his gold, which had been confiscated as a fine, was returned.

It was logical that the first historic and significant breakthrough in the application of science to criminal investigative work should take place in the middle of the nineteenth century. This was a period marked by rapid development in the natural sciences, and in consequence those involved in the criminal justice system turned to the laboratory.

Of lasting importance were the contributions made at this time by Dr. Hans Gross, a former Austrian magistrate turned criminologist, who gained wide recognition as the father of scientific techniques in crime detection. There were other pioneers in other countries, but major attention was focused on Gross's notable advances. He was the forerunner of Alphonse Bertillon of Paris, who later startled the world with the development of anthropometry, a method of identifying offenders by an intricate system of bodily measurements.

Gross's achievements were preceded, however, by the work of a few farsighted men of earlier days, scholars like Lambert Adolphe Quetelet, a noted Belgian statistician and astronomer, who aroused wide interest by his announcement that no two human bodies were exactly alike in dimensions and appearance, just as no two leaves or snowflakes are exactly alike.

At about the same time, progress was being made in the development of new photographic processes to shorten the time required to take pictures of prisoners and the scenes of crimes. Before this, the subjects were sketched by an artist's hand. Invention of the dry plate by an English physician named Maddox soon antiquated the process of the earlier M. Daguerre, whose daguerreotypes on tin were difficult and slow to produce. By 1854, dry plates were being used extensively in prison work in Switzerland.

There were also other pioneers in the investigation field, but widespread attention did not come until 1883 when Bertillon, after long and tenacious efforts in the face of repeated rebuffs and ridicule, succeeded in winning acceptance of his system of body measurements by the French Sûreté.

Before this, while Bertillon was still pressing his pleas for recognition, two men in far separated parts of the world were pioneering, unknown to each other, the use of fingerprints for the solution of crimes and the capture of offenders. Their ultimate accomplishments, influenced by a fateful technical error made by Bertillon in a case of worldwide interest, led to the acceptance of the newer science of fingerprinting, which became known as dactylography, and the recognition of its major importance in police work — an advance of perhaps even greater significance than the method introduced by the widely acclaimed Frenchman.

The early pioneers must not be forgotten, but our concern now turns to those technicians whose skills and resourcefulness led to the present use of the natural sciences in the crime laboratory as well as to the mysteries that motivated them in their advances. We will also examine some more recent cases involving the use of similar sciences.

Chapter 2

Time Brings Progress

I T IS AN INTERESTING COINCIDENCE that Sir Arthur Conan
Doyle's mythical detective, Sherlock Holmes, should have
turned public interest to scientific crime detection in the same
era that a widely acclaimed Austrian criminalist, Dr. Hans
Gross, reached the peak of his career in that field.

Holmes made his first appearance in Conan Doyle's literary
ventures in about 1887, but it remains questionable whether
the creation of the fictional detective was influenced by what
the author had learned of Gross's publicized achievements.
Nevertheless, since Sir Arthur had spent his early years as a
practicing physician, it would have been relatively simple for
him to have introduced into his books his own techniques and
procedures, which he attributed to Holmes.

Gross, born in 1847, devoted himself to his chosen work
until his death in 1915. However, at the age of forty-six he
attained the height of international fame by publishing *A
Handbook of Examining Magistrates*, a volume dealing
primarily with criminal investigations. In 1907 the German
original was translated into English.

Interestingly, it was in 1893, the year of the first appearance
of Gross's published work, that Conan Doyle admitted he had
tired of Holmes as a protagonist and would have put his
hawk-nosed sleuth to rest but for the public demand for more.
There still are those who believe that the popularity of Gross's
scientific work was due in considerable measure to the fanciful
accomplishments of Sherlock Holmes, which convinced many
of the value of the laboratory in crime detection.

While Gross was steeped in study and research in Austria,
another pioneer, an Italian, was devoting himself to a study of
the criminal, the causes of lawless tendencies, hereditary and
environmental influences.

Sir Arthur Conan Doyle

This man was Cesare Lombroso, often referred to as "the father of the science of criminology." Born in Verona in 1836 of Jewish parents, he was writing on technical subjects while still in his teens. As a professor of psychiatry, in 1862 he turned his attention to criminality, contending that criminal ways were inherited — the result of atavism or a reversion to the evil weaknesses either of early forebears or immediate antecedents. He insisted that most habitual offenders bore distinguishing physical characteristics like thin upper lips, unusually protruding ears, long arms, and definite peculiarities in brain structure. Climate and working conditions, he held, were also contributing factors.

Lombroso's interest in the subject had an unusual beginning. Working with the police, he had participated in the difficult capture of an incorrigible highway robber, one Villella, with a long record of lawlessness. After the man's execution, Lombroso undertook an examination of the skull and discovered a small dent on the inside of one of the bones at the nape of Villella's neck. Then he turned to an external study of the heads of prison inmates and concluded that the worst habitual criminals had the skulls and other bodily characteristics of apes.

This was at a time when Darwin's theory of the evolution of the species was attracting wide attention, and Lombroso's conclusions, expounded in a number of books, became the subject of heated discussion. He was challenged by many, including Gross, who declared, "The truth is that there is neither criminal born nor a type of criminal." Though others were more brutal in their criticism, later writers have paid high tribute to Lombroso's studies, crediting him with having opened many minds to new facets of the crime problem.

It was a period for serious thinking on the entire subject, especially in the field of social justice. A century before, another famous Italian, Cesare Becarria, who opposed capital punishment and torturous punishments, had cried out against inhuman penalties. So great an impact did Becarria make in his time that in 1768 a chair of political philosophy was created for him in Milan.

Gross progressed beyond Lombroso's field of criminology, gaining recognition as the father of the new science that he called criminalistics and defined as "the application of techniques from the physical sciences and psychology to the problems of identification and apprehension." He apparently was the first to comprehend that the new laboratory techniques he was developing along crude lines belonged to a field quite different from recognized criminology, a field that concerned itself broadly with the nature of crime as a social problem, penal treatment, punishment, rehabilitation, and police administration.

At an early age Gross undertook the study of law and later became an examining magistrate with a deep-rooted concern for criminal law and crime. In time he was appointed a professor of penal law at the University of Graz, Austria. Unlike many others of his time, he had imagination, insight, and a craving for learning that convinced him of the need for new basic outlooks and procedures that would take the place of the antiquated concepts of criminology.

He realized that the methods of identification in use at the time were largely ineffective. Science, he contended, could solve most crimes if intelligently applied, and he dreamed of the day when this would be achieved. However, trained only in the law, he knew practically nothing of the natural sciences, but he was determined to delve into as many fields as he could in order to put his theories into practice.

His studies continued for more than twenty years, during which time he became knowledgeable in chemistry, physics, photography, microscopy, botany, and zoology. Thus equipped, he set about putting his newly acquired knowledge into practical use in criminal investigations. He successfully tested many of his theories and established the soundness of what he had been advocating. Although his scientific beginnings were a far cry from today's advanced techniques, they did open the way for steady progress.

His subsequent solutions of perplexing cases attracted the attention of his contemporaries, who listened to his reports with amazement. In one instance he brought about the conviction of a burglar who had sworn that a fingernail scar had been made six months before his arrest. Gross proved the man a liar by citing the growth rate of human nails, proving that if the scar was as old as the accused claimed it would have disappeared before his capture. In other cases he demonstrated the value of dust on shoes and fingernail scrapings as vital clues.

As time passed, Gross felt the need to share his experiences and expertise with others. He set to work on his *Criminal Investigation*, an exhaustive volume that reveals the author's surprising knowledge of his subject at the time and the depth of his understanding. In this book, which has been translated into many languages and still is studied today, Gross endeavored to guide law officials in the scientific procedures to be followed in criminal investigations; to illustrate how chemistry, zoology, botany, toxicology, ballistics, and other sciences could be used effectively. He pointed out, for example, how bullets should be examined under the microscope. He elaborated on ways of distinguishing bloodspots from other stains and on the early study of handwriting. Poisons received his serious attention, and he demonstrated the value of astronomy in checking the truth of witnesses who referred to the position of the sun and moon at specified times.

He wrote extensively on the ways of burglars and other offenders, their methods of disguise, and their superstitions. Even their jargon was not overlooked; for example, the writer listed popular usages such as the word "whizzers" for pickpockets.

Above all, Gross sought to impress on investigators the importance of minute scrutiny of the scene of every crime, pioneering the theory, long since followed, that every offender leaves a clue behind him — a telltale something that can be made to divulge vital information. He ever admonished lawmen always to rip open the seams of discarded garments in the search for evidence — perhaps a hidden note. And he stressed the importance of expert medical advice in puzzling death mysteries, a forerunner of today's frequent use of forensic medicine.

Strangely, Gross did not gain a full understanding of Bertillon's work with body measurements until 1888, five years after it had been adopted by the French Sûreté. He soon became convinced of its value, however, and in 1892 he urged his government to follow Frances lead, but ten years were to pass before the Austrian Minister of the Interior directed that a "Bertillon office" be established in Vienna.

Early in March 1879, Bertillon, the eccentric, ill-tempered and unsocial son of a noted and influential physician, Dr. Louis Adolphe Bertillon, had accepted a most unimportant clerkship in the headquarters of the French Sûreté, the investigative branch of the police system, which was then undergoing vital changes. Almost half a century had passed since the resignation of Eugene Vidocq, an ex-convict and jail breaker, who had first established the Sûreté at the height of a crime wave and ruled effectively over a force composed mostly of former convicts. He has been credited with the creation of the first well-organized detective system on the Continent.

From the start Bertillon found his work boring and worthless. He was filing large quantities of information about law-breakers but he concluded that this was of no value, since they continually assumed other names and often changed their outward appearance.

The idea destined to win Bertillon worldwide fame came to him one dull morning only months after he had assumed his work. He had read of the Belgian statistician, Quetelet, and was greatly impressed by the contention that no two human beings were precisely alike in anatomical dimensions.

If that was so, Bertillon reasoned, "Why was it not possible to record the body measurements of criminals for their identification when arrested and even for their apprehension?

What he did not know was that in 1860, when he was a boy of six, Warden Stevens of the prison in Louvain, Belgium was measuring heads, ears, feet, arms, and other parts of his prisoners. Little attention was paid to Stevens, and Bertillon has been recognized as the originator of the system.

Perhaps it is as well that Bertillon did not know. Having realized the potential of his ideas, he was devoting all his spare time to developing a system that would put his theory into practice. Initially, he conceived a method involving eleven major measurements — the head, torso, limbs, hands, and so on. Thoroughly convinced that he had evolved a revolutionary and workable plan, the twenty-six-year-old clerk put his proposal on paper and mailed it to Louis Andrieux, who had succeeded Vidocq as prefect of police.

The reply that Bertillon awaited impatiently did not come, and a short time later he sent a considerably amplified communication. This time he was summoned to Andrieux's office, but if he expected to be greeted with acclaim he was sorely disappointed.

The prefect took a dim view of the young man's ideas. In fact, he declared that the papers he had tried to read were incomprehensible and silly. Bertillon tried to explain, but he was extremely poor in self-expression and the more he spoke the more irritated his listener became. In the end he was rudely told to devote his time to his work under penalty of dismissal.

It was not long before Dr. Bertillon, a man of wide political and academic influence in Paris, learned of the rebuke to his son and decided to inquire into the cause. He went directly to Andrieux, who scornfully thrust the young man's papers into the father's hands. The doctor scanned them and a look of surprise came over his face. "This is something wonderful," he exclaimed excitedly. "This will revolutionize the work of the police."

The prefect, however, was not impressed; he stubbornly refused to alter his previous decision. Dr. Bertillon sent for his son, whom he had previously regarded as a failure, and encouraged him to continue developing the new method. "What good will it do?" the son asked dejectedly.

"Some day there will be a new prefect," Dr. Bertillon replied. "We must have patience."

Three tantalizing years passed before Andrieux left office. Young Bertillon, with scant hope, had spent the time in further work on his system. By now his father was too ill to contact the new prefect, Jean Camescasse, but he had influential friends who undertook to do so. Camescasse listened to them, and though he did not fully understand what they were saying, he agreed to send for Bertillon and give him a chance.

A few days later young Bertillon was in the prefect's office, but he soon sensed the meaning of the conditions under which he would be permitted to demonstrate his innovation. He was told that he would be given two helpers and allowed three months to prove that his method could identify a single prisoner as a repeat offender. As he listened to this challenge he realized its implications. He knew that he had been given a herculean task, probably in the belief that he would fail and be forced to abandon his ideas. But Bertillon was not one to give up easily.

He set to work with feverish haste, recording the measurements of offenders on cards that he carefully checked day after day, comparing them with those of new prisoners brought before him — but to no avail. There were no matching cards.

Weeks slipped by, during which Bertillon did most of his work at home at night, distrusting the two assistants who were ridiculing him behind his back.

When only seven days remained of his three months trial period, Bertillon went into a frenzy, fearing the worst, but good fortune was to smile on him in the nick of time. The break he had been praying for came with the arrival of a certain prisoner who said his name was Dupont.

To Bertillon's searching eyes there was something familiar about the man, yet he feared another disappointment. He examined one file of cards after another. At last he found that the newcomer's measurements matched those of a man named Martin, who had been arrested two months before for theft. "Dupont" angrily admitted his true identity. Elated over this last minute achievement, Bertillon quickly reported it to Camescasse, who grasped the significance of what he had been told. He instructed Bertillon to continue his work with no further time limits and assigned additional men to help him.

Success did not immediately end the ridicule by old-school detectives, but they gradually came to acknowledge the value of Bertillon's new method, especially after he identified scores of former convicts in a relatively short time.

His accomplishments soon became front page news and his name a household word. And as he came to be hailed as the discoverer of a new science in police work, Camescasse suddenly decided that it was time for him to take credit for "finding" so clever an aide.

At his order an identification bureau was established as a branch of the Sûreté and Bertillon was named as its director, with a suite of offices at his disposal. Soon afterward his method was instituted in every French prison, and police throughout the country were ordered to have every prisoner measured in accordance with Bertillon's procedures.

In his first year of official operation, he identified as old offenders forty-nine men and women who had given false names upon rearrest; ten years later the number had grown to 689.

But Bertillon, now virtually a hero, was not content to rest on his laurels. Looking ahead, he soon realized the need to improve his methods to give the policeman on the streets a graphic mental picture of a wanted man. Accordingly, he began placing arrested men and women before the camera, taking both frontal and profile views. Then he developed a way of augmenting these with mental pictures — *portraits parlant* he called them — amplified by coded letters, words, and phrases that revealed distinctive feature's about a head and face.

Bertillon's fame soon spread far beyond French borders. To his great delight, Germany and other neighboring countries began to adopt his method, which had been given the name of bertillonage. The New York police installed it in 1895. If anything were needed to further aggrandize the one-time clerk, it came early in 1892 at a time when every resource of the French police was thrown into the nationwide hunt for a man named Ravachol, wanted for bombing the Paris residence of a judge who had recently given severe prison sentences to a group of anarchists. At the time anarchistic violence was terrifying all of France.

Through the help of a *mouton*, as the police called their informers, suspicion fell on a radical named Chaumartin, who confessed that although he had planned the crime the bomb had actually been placed by Ravachol. While every resource of the Sûreté was being strained in the search for the wanted man, word came from a nearby city that an old offender named François C. Koenigstein, wanted for murder, had often used the alias Ravachol.

Now Bertillon, whose bureau had photographed and measured Koenigstein when he had been arrested long before, produced a detailed description of the man. This was broadcast with his photograph immediately in all parts of France. Special attention was given to a scar on Koenigstein's left thumb.

It was a detail that proved to be of the utmost importance. Two weeks later a man with a similar scar was observed eating in a Paris café. Police quickly surrounded the place and the protesting patron was arrested. In less than an hour he was identified by Bertillon as the wanted Koenigstein alias Ravachol. The story electrified the country and Bertillon's fame seemed to know no bounds.

With surprising frequency Bertillon's method continued to solve the most baffling mysteries, as in the case of a wealthy woman known to possess a fortune in government bonds who was found murdered in her Paris home. Robbery was not considered to be the motive until detectives uncovered a secret hiding place under the bedroom floor. It was empty.

Police reasoned that the killer must have been a trusted friend who knew of her cache, and suspicion turned to a handsome, well-known physician with a long gray beard. Neighbors in describing him told of a peculiar lump on the bridge of his nose.

After four months of intensive search, an officer, thumbing through Bertillon's records, came upon a photograph of a man whose nose was similarly marked. He was in prison in Brest for robbery, but those who knew the handsome doctor said that the picture was of another person, especially since the subject in the picture was clean shaven. However, when inquiries were made at the prison, it became known that the robber, in requesting medicine, was using terms that would be known only to a physician.

The suspect was transferred to Paris, where he was made to let his beard grow. He was then identified as the wanted man and confessed that he had turned to robbery, deliberately bungling his crime in the belief that a murderer would be safe in a prison cell. The stolen bonds were found hidden in his home.

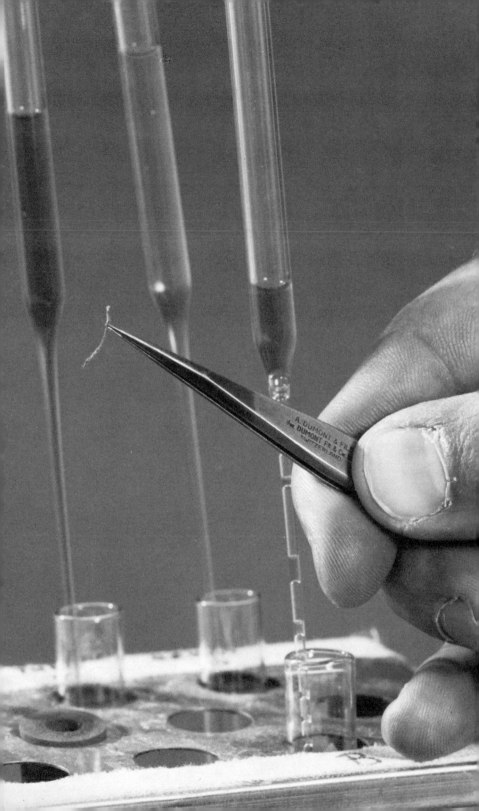

Chapter 3
America's Sherlock Holmes

MANY LAYMEN, fascinated by crime mysteries, are intrigued by the work of the pioneer criminalists, as discussed in earlier chapters.

Most of them wonder if the work of these pioneers has helped Twentieth Century experts in scientific crime detection, and if so, who have those criminalists been and what have they accomplished in actual practice?

The late Luke S. May was one of those criminalists who did avail himself of these earlier beginnings and subsequent progress.

For more than forty years Luke S. May was known throughout the Pacific Northwest as "America's Sherlock Holmes." He earned the sobriquet by his unusual feats of crime detection, utilizing his wide knowledge of the natural sciences to unravel baffling enigmas in both criminal and civil cases.

To his laboratories in Seattle, Washington, law enforcement officers, corporation lawyers, and government officials came from all parts of the United States and Canada to seek his help in investigations that required his unusual versatility in chemistry, ballistics, physics, biology, and other sciences. He was an authority on fingerprints and handwriting, and he was thoroughly familiar with the techniques of electrical and mechanical engineering. These skills he utilized in a widely diversified range of cases covering practically every major crime in the statutes. With the aid of his microscopes he could make a tiny thread or a minute wooden fibre tell an amazing story.

Once May used a little fir needle to weave a web of evidence that sent a murderer to the gallows. On another occasion, he ended a $900,000 will contest by proving that the vital signatures were forgeries. And he freed a soldier held for the murder of a well-known merchant by disclosing that the man was a

With the aid of his microscope, May could make a tiny thread tell an amazing story.

suicide and not the victim of bandits as the police had concluded.

Like many others in his field, he was as proud of his accomplishments in clearing the innocent as he was of his record in sending the guilty to prison. Although death ended his notable career in 1965, he still holds a significant place in the top ranks of his unique profession.

Luke May was scarcely thirteen when he decided to make criminal investigation his life's work. He started out four years later and his private practice was interrupted only once — in 1933 when he was drafted to reorganize the Seattle Detective Bureau. He had cleared up 1,400 percent more burglary cases than had previously been solved.

A slender, baldish man with clean-cut features and clear, piercing eyes, May believed that no one commits a crime without leaving at least one clue to his or her identity. Discovery of that clue and its interpretation, however, are not always simple.

In one of his most celebrated cases, May solved a perplexing murder mystery because as a chemist he knew that ammonia discolors human flesh after death — a little detail that a conniving killer had overlooked. May often recalled the case because, more than any other in his career, it demonstrated how an experienced investigator could vindicate an innocent man caught in the meshes of circumstance and suspicion. Moreover, he succeeded in sending the murderer to the scaffold.

The innocent man was Dr. Fred Covell, a highly respected chiropractor from Bandon, Oregon, a devoted husband and the dutiful father of four children by his first marriage.

It was Friday morning, September 3, 1923 when Dr. Covell, busy in his office, was called away from a patient to answer the telephone. Picking up the receiver, he quickly recognized the excited voice of his forty-six-year-old brother, Arthur, a bedridden invalid who for years had occupied an upstairs room in the large, comfortable Covell home. "Come home quickly," Arthur Covell cried. "Something terrible has happened to Ebba."

Knowing that his wife was subject to sudden illness and had been in a despondent mood, Dr. Covell pressed for details, but his brother seemed too agitated to answer coherently, so the harried husband threw off his gown, reached for his coat, and hurried to his car. The ride home, a considerable distance, seemed interminable despite the light traffic that enabled him to drive rapidly and to take the short cuts with which he was familiar. Nevertheless, it was fully half an hour later that he pulled up in front of his house and hurried in. He found his wife lying still across her bed. Anxiously he looked at the glassy eyes and grabbed for her pulse. It did not take him long to know that she was dead.

"What in the world happened to Ebba?" he called frantically to his invalid brother.

"I haven't the faintest idea," the other answered, speaking from his bed in the adjoining room. "Two of the children found her lying on the kitchen floor. I told them to lift her on to the bed as best they could. Then I called you."

Dr. Covell phoned for the family physician, who arrived soon afterward and examined the body. He could not tell whether death was due to a heart attack or to other causes. Her husband, recalling her melancholia, suggested that she might have taken her own life, yet the body showed no visible evidence of poison and they could find none in the kitchen or in the bedroom. But in the medicine cabinet they found a half-empty vial of sleeping pills, which strengthened their suspicion of suicide. Finally they notified the coroner, who in turn called the sheriff's office.

Since the cause of death was undetermined, the body was removed to the coroner's office, and Sheriff Ed Ellington of Coos County, who came to the house with his deputy, Sam Malehorn, began questioning the grief-stricken husband and the two older children. Dr. Covell told them that his wife had appeared to be in fair health when he left for his office a few hours before he received his brother's call. The two older children, Alton, a mentally retarded boy of sixteen, and his sister, Lucille, two years younger, were interviewed, but they could only say that entering the house from play they had found their stepmother on the floor and had called their uncle. The other children, somewhat younger, had been away at the time.

Unexpected developments followed the coroner's order for a postmortem examination, which Dr. Covell and the authorities believed would verify their suspicions of suicide. To the amazement of everyone, the autopsy surgeon reported that

Mrs. Covell had died of a broken neck. This conclusion, he said, was reached after he had made an incision that disclosed fractured vertebrae.

Almost at once suspicion turned on Dr. Covell, the authorities reasoning that since he was an experienced chiropractor with large, powerful hands, he would have been capable of inflicting such injuries in a way that would leave no external evidence. An element of time even strengthened their mistrust. Although the exact hour of Mrs. Covell's death could not be accurately determined, the coroner believed it would have been possible for her husband to have killed her before leaving for his office.

Interrogated along those lines, Dr. Covell at first seemed so dumbfounded at even being suspected that he could not take the officers seriously. It was not until they pressed their questions that he fully realized his situation. He spoke tearfully of his devotion to his ailing wife and insisted that any thought of murder was absurd. He was certain that her death must have occurred during his absence.

Still far from satisfied, the sheriff and his deputy withdrew, prepared to keep the husband under surveillance pending a coroner's inquest. When this took place several days later, the autopsy surgeon reported his findings. There was routine testimony concerning the finding of the body, and the jury returned a verdict that the fatal injury had resulted from causes "still to be determined." The authorities were called on to press a vigorous inquiry.

Dr. Covell was grilled for hours, and once more his profession was emphasized in support of police suspicion. He readily countered all their suspicions except one. He could not account for his wife's broken neck, but he surmised that it might have been sustained in a fall. The officers, however, insisted — and probably rightly — that a fall of such severity would have resulted in external bruises. For this he had no explanation.

Meanwhile, feeling throughout the county was running high. The mystery of Mrs. Covell's death had become front page news, and people were sharply divided in their judgment. Friends and acquaintances of the husband were certain of his innocence. Others, quick to condemn, turned against him. The next move was up to the authorities, and they did not wait long after the funeral to arrest Dr. Covell.

In his jail cell Dr. Covell still protested his innocence and sent for a lawyer. Days of intensive investigation followed, but the officers admitted they were making no headway. They were certain that they had not made a mistake, yet they agreed that it would be difficult to convince a jury. Sheriff Ellington and District Attorney Ben Fisher conferred again, wondering what their next move should be.

"I'm going to send for Luke May," the prosecutor finally announced. "He's cleared up other cases as tough as this. Maybe he can help us now."

The criminalist was contacted in his Seattle laboratory and soon was on his way to Oregon. But as he hurried southward in his car, he little realized how extraordinary a case confronted him — a case in which the stars and planets were to play strange roles and a hypnotist was to cast a sinister spell.

Arriving in Bandon, May sat down with District Attorney Fisher and listened to the case he now was called on to solve.

"We want the truth," Fisher told him. "If Dr. Covell is guilty we must develop our case so that a jury will accept it. If he's innocent, we certainly want to know it and we must find the murderer, whoever he is. Can you go to work right now?"

May agreed. "My first step," he began, "will be to question the man you're holding. Can that be arranged?"

A few hours later he was talking to Dr. Covell in the jail, and when the interview was over May was convinced that the man was telling the truth. This conclusion he promptly reported to the district attorney, and the two discussed their next move. The officers had already eliminated the bedridden Arthur Covell, agreeing that it would have been physically impossible for him to have killed his sister-in-law. They were equally convinced that the boy, Alton, was not involved, and earlier inquiry had eliminated the possibility that a stranger had been admitted to the house or had broken in. How then had Ebba Covell met her death? Was she actually murdered or could she have died of an accidental fall?

After a time May announced the steps he proposed to follow. "I want an order to exhume the body as quickly as possible," he said "and I want to talk to those children. After that I'm going to search the house inch by inch."

A prolonged questioning of the children turned out to be futile. Alton insisted that he had already told all he knew.

However, he volunteered the information that some weeks before he had been committed to a school for retarded children but that his admission had been delayed because the place was overcrowded. May asked himself whether this could be significant.

The following day the woman's body was taken from the grave and moved to the coroner's office. May had learned how the autopsy surgeon had reached his conclusions, and, with his own knowledge of such work, he questioned the doctor's findings. The surgeon, he was told, had simply inserted a finger into an incision in the back of the woman's neck and had concluded it was fractured because the head moved forward. To check his doubts, May sent for a noted authority on postmortems, Dr. Mingus of Marshfield, Oregon, with whom he had worked many times.

In the dismal autopsy room, May stood beside Dr. Mingus as the doctor engaged in a minute examination of the body. Slowly the surgeon shook his head. "The neck very definitely is not broken," he announced. "Someone has made a bad mistake." Then the two turned to a minute examination of the remains. May spoke next. He pointed out some curious dark red splotches about the mouth and nose and on one cheek.

"Peculiar things, these," he remarked. "Looks to me like ammonia came in contact with her face. It discolors the skin, you know, after death. How could . . . ?"

"You're right," Dr. Mingus exclaimed. "Let's proceed with the usual checks."

They subjected the skin to various eliminating chemical tests and soon agreed that May's suspicions were correct, yet they could only wonder what connection this could possibly have with the mystery before them. Certainly it called for more intensive investigation, but they agreed that their discovery should be kept secret while they sought an answer. May's next move was to drive to the Covell home and begin the minute search he had intended. Before long he made an amazing disclosure. To his astonishment, he discovered evidence that eventually was to reveal Arthur Covell, the cripple, as an experienced astrologist and a hypnotist of extraordinary power, practicing from his bed and his wheelchair.

The detective's first surprising find was Arthur Covell's diary, written largely with the help of astrological signs. May had just begun to examine the cryptic writing when he came upon a baffling entry. Though it had been made five days after Mrs. Covell's death, it recorded the writer's doings on the date of her demise — details of his breakfast, his reading of the newspapers, and similar incidents. May thought it strange that there was no mention of the tragic happening of that day.

Elsewhere in the room were curious charts and papers, describing the planets and the stars and interpreting them and their positions in terms of human destiny. There was also correspondence showing that from his bed Arthur Covell had drafted the horoscopes of Hollywood celebrities and influential New Yorkers, sending them to these individuals and exchanging letters. In some way, possibly through newspaper reports, May had learned that Hollywood celebrities had complained of receiving crank horoscope correspondence.

All this May confided to the authorities and a new line of inquiry was begun. Two days later unexpected circumstances played into their hands. With Dr. Covell in jail, it had been necessary to move his invalid brother to the county farm, where he could receive proper care. Although this had been done, Deputy Sheriff Malehorn, who has been assigned to work with May, learned that the cripple before leaving home had asked a neighbor to take a box of horoscopes with him for safekeeping. When this container was examined it proved to be a real Pandora's box. It was crammed with scribbled notes, which at first glance appeared to be only vague plots for fiction stories, but interspersed between the scrawled lines were the names of various prominent people. Fastened to some of the notes were other slips with astrological characters evenly spaced as though they were intended to form words. May and the deputy, concluding that these involved a code, set out to decipher it. Days later, when they had finally found the key, they were appalled by what they read. The cryptic notes proved to be instructions to the nephew, Alton, to commit a series of cold-blooded murders!

In all, twenty-nine men and women, some of them prominent in the region, had been marked for death. In each case the lunar destinies of the intended victim were described, with astrological readings that detailed the exact day and hour on which to strike. Different methods were indicated, and minute instructions were provided should the carefully made plans miscarry. And finally they came upon the horoscope of Ebba Covell with a note determining the time for her to die. It was the exact day of her murder!

May lost no time in conferring with the officials, and the doors of the jail soon opened for the innocent chiropractor, who had feared that he was really doomed. Realizing they had arrested an innocent man, the police were quick to pursue their latest clues. Soon they discovered that the invalid brother, working always from his bed, had connived with a ring of swindlers to dupe unsuspecting victims. In a continuous chain of correspondence, he had mailed horoscopes intended to show the exact time for making profitable investments. On the designated day, a confederate would call on the individual, offering sure-fire investments, which of course, were worthless. The clique was obviously, reaping rich profits.

Alton and his sister, Lucille, were brought before May and the officers for further questions. Both denied knowing anything of their uncle's plotting, but it was obvious now that they were concealing something. The two children revealed a fondness for "Uncle Artie," as they called him, and seemed indifferent toward their father. Lucille in fact said she firmly believed he had killed their stepmother. The uncle, the authorities had already learned, had often practiced hypnotism, and it now became apparent that he had exercised his powers over the two youngsters.

May and Malehorn went to the county farm to confront the crippled Arthur, but they soon realized that they were contending with a stubborn, defiant man. He stared at them with his deep black, penetrating eyes, and the two visitors exchanged knowing glances, realizing that he was trying to exert his hypnotic powers.

"We know all about you," May began. "We've cracked your code. Now's the time for you to come clean. Come on — we're listening."

Arthur gazed at them sharply but his expression remained unchanged. "What of it?" he finally blurted out.

"None of that stuff," May snapped; then for a few moments he stood silently, staring back at the bedridden man.

When he spoke again it was with slow, clipped words. "You murdered Ebba — we know that — and you got Alton to do it for you. Now listen carefully — you plotted to kill E. J. Pressy,

his wife, and their three children. We know all about your
plans to kill Ira Sidwell. We know everything. Now talk."
    A faint smile came over the crippled man's face. He wet his
lips and began to speak. "You've got me all wrong," he began,
speaking softly with surprising calm. "Yes, I did write out plots
for killing people but I was only working my imagination over-
time to keep from getting bored. I guess you'd call it fantasy. I
just got a kick out of writing this kind of stuff, but really I
didn't intend it seriously. Why should I want to kill anybody?
And how could I — even if I wanted to?"
    "Then you did write this stuff?" May pressed.
    "Only for fun — for my own amusement, like I said. It was
my way of passing the time away."
    The two men questioned him for hours but he could not be
shaken. Stubbornly he insisted that he had no part in Mrs.
Covell's death, that he certainly had no knowledge of how it
had occurred. At last May and his companion withdrew, now
thoroughly convinced of Arthur's guilt but aware that he was
far from ready to confess.
    After much discussion they came upon a plan to wring the
truth from him, but first May wanted to continue his check of
Alton's movements in the days before his stepmother's death.
He already strongly suspected that the boy was seriously
involved. Earlier days spent in interviewing Alton's friends
had been fruitless, and careful inquiry into his actions had also
produced no incriminating information. Now the investigator
resumed his task, more determined than ever, but a considerable time was to elapse before he would uncover a worthwhile
clue.
    May began a systematic check of the stores within a wide
radius of the boy's home. The work was discouraging until at
last he walked into a small grocery and began with his routine
questions — did they know Alton Covell and had he made any
purchases there lately?
    The grocer knew the lad and remembered his last visit well.
"It was close to a month ago," he recalled, little suspecting the
importance of what he was about to tell. "He came running in
here and bought a bottle of ammonia. As I remember it now, he
seemed somewhat excited, but you know how kids are."
    That was all May needed to hear, but there were still many
missing pieces to the puzzle. Obviously Alton had played a role

in his stepmother's death, but what that role was still required a definite answer. Again May conferred with the sheriff, and they decided to proceed with a scheme they had been considering.

Taking newspaper editors into his confidence, May told them of Arthur Covell's admission that he had scribbled plans for wholesale murder, although he had denied any intention of carrying them out. The newsmen jumped at the chance, for here was an opportunity not only to cooperate with the authorities but to print a sensational story as well. "Crippled Astrologer Plans Murder" read one glaring headline the next morning. "Arthur Covell Confesses to Planning Murders" another paper announced, with some stretch of the truth. This was exactly what May wanted.

He promptly took the newspapers to the Covell house and told Alton to read the headlines. The investigator deliberately concealed the story itself, since he wanted the boy to believe that his uncle had confessed to the murder of Ebba Covell.

"Come now, Alton, tell us all about it," May demanded, but the boy merely shrugged his shoulders, just as he had days before when he had been asked about the ammonia purchase.

"I told you I don't know nothin' about it," he repeated. When prolonged questioning failed to shake him, May notified the sheriff and the boy was led away to jail.

In the next few days May and Sheriff Ellington, working with a picked force of deputies, made more startling disclosures. They learned that for some time Arthur Covell, despite his infirmities, had exerted a strange hypnotic influence over his nephew — a power that seemed to compel the youth to do the older man's bidding. Of late Alton had been sending secret messages to his uncle, his practice being to paste magazine pages together and to scribble notes on the margins of the glued leaves. Ellington found several of these in the cripple's room. All of them referred to the murder investigation.

The sheriff discovered also that Arthur was sending notes to his nephew, hiding them in the cores of apples. By this means the boy was warned to say nothing to the authorities.

On the afternoon of October 9, more than a month after his stepmother's death, Alton Covell was brought to the sheriff's office and questioned again without result. Exasperated, May finally handed him a sheet of paper and a pen, telling him to return to his cell and write whatever he had to say. He came back half an hour later with a scribbled note that simply repeated his previous statements.

"Go back there again and think it over," May snapped angrily. "Think hard, and see if you can't clear your mind of everything that's troubling you. Then you can start your life all over again — you're young and you have a long time ahead of you."

Alton returned to his cell. An hour later he sent out word that he wanted to see May and Ellington again. When they met a short time later, Alton handed the two a carefully written note, one of the frankest and most extraordinary confessions they had ever seen. Brazenly admitting that he had followed his uncle's directions in snuffing out his stepmother's life with ammonia, the boy had written the following:

> I want to start and lead a clean life, and I want to be able to look back on everything I do and not be ashamed of anything I will do in the future. I don't know what made me do it. I can't understand why I done such a thing. I will see that it never happens again. I want to look back on a clear trail.
>
> I put ammonia on a rag and Ebba was standing by the stove. I walked up to her from behind and on the right-hand side. I put the rag over her nose with my right hand and held her arms with my left. I held it on her nose for about three minutes after I let her down on the floor. There was a little ammonia left in the bottle and I threw it down into the gulch.
>
> Then I went and told my uncle that I had done it. Lucille and my uncle knew about the plan first. My uncle was the first to tell me. He told me to get the ammonia and how to use it.

The note was sent to the foreman of the grand jury, and a group of officials, working with May, prepared to confront Arthur Covell with his nephew's statement. The party composed of Sheriff Ellington, Deputy Malehorn, District Attorney Fisher, and May, had agreed to follow the same strategy that had finally wrung the truth from Alton. Fisher was chosen to be their spokesman.

"Your nephew, Alton, has told us everything," he began, as the men took their places around the cripple's bed at the

county farm. "I'm not asking you any questions now. Just
think it over — and write down anything you've got to say.
We'll be back in a day or so for your answer."

Early the next morning the grand jury foreman was advised
that Arthur Covell had a written statement ready. He hastened
to the farm, walked anxiously into the invalid's room, and was
handed a sheaf of papers. He scanned them eagerly and read the
following:

> I make this a voluntary statement. I alone was the one
> to plan the details and select the day. Lucille had noth-
> ing to do with the plan or its execution.
>
> Both Alton and Lucille were at all times under control
> of my mind and will. My will was their will. They never
> resisted my influence, but done without question as I
> wished it done. They never argued, or thought if the ac-
> tion was right or wrong, but my influence over both was
> so complete they seemed incapable to resist or think in-
> dependently beyond my wish.
>
> In regard to Ebba, soon after moving upstairs, I told
> Alton I wanted her out of the way. I told him how to do it
> without violence or bloodshed and with ammonia. I told
> him I would choose the day, that I would not force him
> to do it, and if he wanted to refuse it was all right with
> me; but as I said this, I knew in my own heart he
> couldn't help doing as I wanted.
>
> My brother, Fred, is entirely innocent. Lucille is inno-
> cent of any participation in the crime. Alton as an indi-
> vidual is innocent. I forced my will on him and made
> him act for me; in other words I used his body and his
> strength as though it were my own; he had not the
> power of will to resist me. I alone am guilty of the whole
> thing. I have kept Alton under my control for a great
> many years and it is this which makes him seem not
> bright, sometimes deficient. My last instruction to him
> before we were separated was: "If you get in a tight
> pinch with this and there is no other way out, it will be
> all right with me if you tell how I made you do it. I do
> not want you to suffer for my sake." Hence his and my
> statement.
>
> Alton has a very mild nature, with nothing vicious in

his makeup and if left to his own devices would be incapable of ever taking a human life.

Arthur Covell

Additional guards were immediately stationed in the invalid's room and preparations were started for his trial, but events did not move as easily or as quickly as the authorities had expected. Carried into court on a stretcher, the confessed murderer surprised everyone by pleading not guilty, explaining that he had admitted the crime only to save his nephew. The trial began a few weeks later, and it was not long before Arthur's strange hypnotic spell on the children became apparent.

Young Alton and his sister were called in turn to the witness chair. As the prosecutor began his questions, the defendant was seen staring at them with glaring eyes, and they sat, transfixed and mute, until in each instance the district attorney stepped between the witness and the accused. Only then did the children begin to speak.

The defense made a stirring plea for sympathy, picturing the plight of a man with a broken back and pleading for clemency. At last the jury retired and Arthur Covell awaited its return with an optimism that amazed all who heard him. "The stars will save me," he told them. "The stars are in my favor; wait, you'll see."

His faith in stellar intervention failed, however, for the jury returned a verdict finding him guilty of first-degree murder, and he was sentenced to the gallows. While an appeal was pending, Alton was placed on trial and the jury, deliberating only forty-five minutes, also convicted him of murder. Because of his youth and his mental condition, he was given a sentence of life imprisonment.

The higher courts finally denied his uncle's appeal, and plans for the execution proceeded. Again he insisted that the stars would rescue him, but the governor refused to intercede. When the time for the execution came, guards lifted him into a wheelchair and led him to the scaffold. "I bear no ill will toward anyone," he said, as he stared at the noose close by. "All of you simply did your duty."

"Just why did you do it, Arthur?" someone asked.

"I'm a cripple," he replied, "and I didn't want to be dependent on anyone. I killed Ebba so I could have full control over the children. She was always coming between us. Can't you understand?"

Minutes later he was strapped to a board to keep his body upright and carried to the trap. The hangman, working fast, proceeded with his grisly task.

Chapter 4

Monkey Business

THE STORY OF Dr. Edmond Locard's unique solution of a long series of jewelry thefts in Lyon, France is related by one of his biographers as an example of the rare ingenuity and perceptiveness that established his place among the foremost crime investigators of all time. His brilliant career, extending from about the turn of the century until his retirement in 1951, will be recalled here.

In discussing Locard, note must also be taken of one of his contemporaries already mentioned — Robert Heindl of Germany — for their paths crossed frequently and they fruitfully shared their knowledge and experiences.

Locard, whose direction of the Institute of Criminalistics for the entire Rhone Prefecture attracted worldwide attention, was once called on for help by the Lyon police, who were at their wits' end over a repeated series of thefts of jewelry from wealthy homes. In every instance, the pilfering had taken place in broad daylight, the thief obviously having entered through an open window. Adding further to the mystery was the fact that the intruder took only one piece of jewelry at a time and the loot was always bright and highly polished.

Detectives first attributed the thefts to boys. Numbers of young gangsters were arrested but to no avail. As the thefts continued, the police came under severe criticism and at last it was decided to call on Dr. Locard to take charge.

Having paid close attention to fingerprinting as well as to many other criminal sciences, he first asked to see photographs of all the marks left on the window ledges of the victims. These had already been carefully checked against the records of the Lyon police without result. As Locard studied them under a powerful glass and sometimes microscopically, he discovered that they varied materially from the prints of human fingers; there was a lack of definite patterns.

For a time the expert was puzzled, but after hours in the laboratory he suddenly found the answer.

"These are the prints of a monkey," he exclaimed to an aide. "They can be identified just as human marks can be identified." Then he called for a textbook showing simian handprints and quickly verified his conclusion.

The police were interested but perplexed. "What you say is all very good but how do we go about arresting the guilty monkeys?" one of the officers asked.

"I think I know how to do it," Locard told him. "Just carry out my orders."

In Lyon at the time there were a number of organ-grinders plying their trade, each depending on the help of a well-trained monkey. Locard promptly issued an order directing all these men to appear at headquarters on a morning three days hence and to bring their pets with them. One at a time the monkeys were fingerprinted as Locard looked on and carefully compared each print with the photographed marks left on the windowsills. Before long the expert put an accusing hand on the guilty animal and told its owner that he was under arrest.

The grinder denied his guilt, but a search of his lodgings revealed all the stolen jewelry. He confessed that he had trained his monkey to steal, but only from unoccupied rooms. Why only shiny baubles were taken was obvious.

The organ-grinder went to jail and his pet received a new home in the city's zoo.

However, fingerprinting was not Locard's major interest. He pioneered in a new field — dust. Eager to progress beyond the achievements of Gross and Bertillon, he conceived the idea that all criminals at the scene of the crime had to come into contact with dust, which would then leave some traces in or on their clothing, on their skin, or even under their fingernails. Analyzing that dust, he reasoned, would provide valuable clues if the findings could be accurately interpreted. To this concept he gave tireless attention, and his results justified his confidence.

Born in 1847, he had pursued his advanced studies at the University of Lyon under the celebrated Alexandre Lacassagne, professor of pathology and forensic medicine. He was to become a physician, a chemist, a pathologist, and finally an expert on forgeries. After earning his degrees he traveled extensively for further study before returning to Lyon, eager to put his knowledge to practical use. Appearing before the officials of the Rhone Prefecture in 1910, he urged the creation of a scientific laboratory for police work. He was given a small room, inadequate for his purpose, but he made the most of this facility and proceeded to demonstrate the value of dust as a clue.

It was not long before he was called on to investigate an outbreak of counterfeiting that had plagued the area for a considerable time. A suspect had been arrested but vigorously denied his guilt. Locard obtained the man's clothing, took it to his dingy laboratory, and searched meticulously for dust. Soon he had before him a tray of tiny particles of earth, in which he discovered minute specks of metal — the clue for which he had been hunting. After ascertaining the precise nature of the metallic substance, he traced its source and captured a gang of worthless money makers.

Now confident of the soundness of his theory, he proceeded to study and classify various types of dust. Ten years later his laboratory was crammed with countless specimens of many varieties, taken from the clothing and bodies of offenders. Many of these were classified to indicate the probable occupations and locale of the suspects. On shelves in a separate room stood scores of little bottles containing fingernail scrapings, laboriously gathered by a student whom Locard had interested in this special field. His pupil was Emile Villebrun.

Locard's original one-room laboratory had by this time grown into a university department that attracted students from all parts of the world. His training stressed the importance of dust in investigative work and the need for leaving no stone unturned in the hunt for physical evidence at the scenes of crimes. He often admonished his students to be objective in their work, avoiding preconceived conclusions. In this he frequently quoted Bertillon, who once said, "One can only see what one observes."

Some years after initiating his work with dust, Locard expressed his surprise over his tardiness in developing what proved to be a simple yet effective approach: gathering minute samples of dust from an article of clothing and determining from it which objects the suspect had brushed past and touched. The microscopic particles of dust that cover our bodies and clothing, Locard concluded, are the minute witnesses to each of our movements and encounters.

In this field Locard's work was followed by others and advanced far beyond his earliest expectations. Among them was an Amsterdam chemist, J. C. van Ledden-Hulsebosch, and later Dr. Albert Schneider of Berkeley, California, who in 1910 invented a specially designed vacuum cleaner for gathering dust evidence.

One of Locard's biographers, H.J. Wells, director of the Metropolitan Police Forensic Science Laboratory in London, wrote that the origin of many methods in common use today can be traced to Locard's Institute of Criminalistics, as his laboratory came to be known. Locard also pioneered in dental comparisons. As a handwriting expert he is now recognized as one of the two greatest, the other being the late Albert S. Osborn of New York.

Heindl, mentioned earlier for his research into the origins of criminal identification, was to Germany what Locard was to France. Born in 1883, he became a law student at Munich University. There his studies led to an intensive interest in criminology, and he is said to have been the first person in Germany to recognize the potential values of fingerprinting while that science was in its infancy. He was extremely critical of Bertillon's system, insisting that it deterred the effective use of fingerprints.

After graduation from Munich, he went to London to study the methods of Scotland Yard. Then, returning to his native land, he was appointed head of the crime investigation division of the Dresden police. He won wide recognition as a pioneer in the use of tire marks as identifying clues, which are still important today in many types of crime investigation. In 1931 he published an extensive classification of tire patterns, a forerunner of far more elaborate records now kept by every police department.

Rudolph Reiss ranks with Locard in having furthered many of the advances made by Gross and Bertillon. He is said to have borne a close physical resemblance to the mythical Sherlock Holmes.

Educated at the University of Lausanne, he won a doctorate in both physics and chemistry, but his special skill was with the camera. In fact, he added photography to police science.

His later classes in that subject at Lausanne proved so successful that in 1902 his subject became known for the first time as forensic photography. He devised new techniques for using the camera both in the laboratory and at the scenes of crimes. After a time his department, which had aroused the interest of many top laboratory experts on the Continent, became the Lausanne Institute of Police Science. To it came detectives from many European countries.

Like Locard, he was expert in detecting forgery of important documents. His skill with the camera enabled him to photograph disputed writing under difficult conditions and to establish the genuine from the spurious. He wrote numerous books and papers on various aspects of police science up to the time of his death in 1929.

Chapter 5

Fingerprints: Nature's Signature

W HILE THE INITIAL EFFORTS of criminalists to have fingerprinting accepted as an exact science in crime detection
did not begin until the middle of the nineteenth century,
primitive knowledge of the subject can be traced far back into
antiquity. There is ample evidence that even in biblical times
some people knew that no two individuals had exactly the
same markings on their fingertips. Early Babylonians pressed
their fingers against soft clay to guard against the forgery of
important papers. Chinese emperors in ancient times used
their thumbprints to sign documents, as did those unable to
write their names.

History recognizes four men of later years as pioneers in the
use of fingerprints for criminal identification, although the
principle was known much earlier and applied in a crude way.
One of the first recorded uses of this technique in a criminal
trial occurred in Rome in the first century of the Christian era,
when bloody palm prints on a wall became the pivotal evidence against a blind man accused of killing his father. The
defense counsel, a distinguished lawyer named Quintilian,
challenged this contention, insisting that the stain was made
deliberately by the accused man's stepmother to cast suspicion
on her sightless stepson. The defendant was acquitted.

Centuries afterward, in 1684, an English physician, Dr.
Nehemiah Grew, reported to a group of medical men in London that he had discovered essential differences in fingerprint
patterns. He was followed in Italy two years later by Dr. Mar-
cello Malpighi, a noted anatomist, who made several futile
efforts to interest his colleagues in what he had learned by
comparing fingerprints under a microscope. Even his explanation of the loops and whorls he had perceived failed to impress
his listeners.

Interest in the subject appears to have waned considerably for a number of years, although an English engraver of woodcuts, Thomas Berwick, did gain some attention when he began etching his fingerprints on his works. The next advancement came shortly afterward, when John Evangelist Parkinji, a professor of anatomy at Breslau University, completed his treatise for an advanced medical degree. In it he presented what was perhaps the first move toward the classification of fingerprints. Parkinji's idea was to segregate prints into nine groups, based on patterns of whorls, loops, and arches, but the professor even then did not foresee what value his plan might have in criminal identification.

Fully four decades slipped by until one of those strange coincidences in the advancement of science brought two men to the fore as new pioneers in the use of fingerprints by criminalists.

Neither man knew what the other was doing. One of them was William James Herschel, a grandson of the famous astronomer. He was the chief administrative officer of the Houghly District of Bengal, and he had been devoting all his leisure time to fingerprints and their potential value, having read much about their use in China. He had become convinced that no two people in the world had precisely the same finger marks and that this phenomenon could be used effectively to stop the current practice of forging documents for pensions.

Unknown to Herschel, similar studies were being carried out in Japan by a Scottish physician and surgeon, Dr. Henry Faulds of Taukiji Hospital in Tokyo. Both men had learned in their own way that oil and sweat from the pores in the ridges of fingertips caused latent prints, which usually remained invisible until they were brushed with a chemical powder — a technique still in use today.

Herschel might have remained in ignorance of Faulds's work for a considerably longer time had not Faulds, thinking himself alone in the field, written to a British magazine, *Nature*, explaining his theory and citing its value in apprehending fugitives. This was a big step forward, since Herschel had only advocated the use of prints in identifying lawbreakers once they were behind bars.

The Faulds report was read by Herschel with considerable resentment. He promptly communicated with the publication, telling of his own accomplishments. Now it was Faulds's turn to retaliate. He protested angrily to the British Home Office but, receiving no satisfaction, carried his grievance to Charles Darwin, who had expressed interest in the subject. In response, Darwin suggested that Faulds place the issue in the hands of another pioneer, who was then involved in a study of heredity.

This man, Sir Francis Galton, first inquired independently into the subject; then he met both Herschel and Faulds. He was fascinated by what they told him, although he soon realized that to put their theory to practical use it would be necessary to develop a system whereby prints could be easily and quickly classified for comparison. His first proposal was to divide prints into two major groups — the latent ones, which could be made visible only by chemical treatment, and the others, which were easily observed because they had been made by fingers usually stained with blood or some other substance. From then on Galton evolved a plan for the minute study of loops, arches, and whorls, classifying them into distinct categories on the basis of observable differences.

He was still further developing his system, giving credit to Herschel as the actual pioneer, when a fourth man, Sir Edward Henry, came forward, eager to improve on what the others had done. Before long he had added many new groupings to Galton's original classifications, but he fully realized that a still more practical system was required and that without it police files would probably become so crammed with fingerprints that valuable time would be lost in comparing new ones with those in the records. How to accomplish this challenged his ingenuity.

This question was uppermost in his mind one morning when he took his seat on a train bound for Calcutta. There, pondering the problem, an idea suddenly went flashing through his mind. He reached into his pocket for a card or a piece of paper but there was none. Then, fearing that his thoughts might slip from memory as quickly as they had come, he pulled down his shirt cuffs and scribbled a few brief notes. He had conceived a new procedure calling for prints to be taken from the five fingers of each hand and classified on the basis of five patterns — plain arches, tented arches, whorls, lunar loops, and radial loops. With this as a starting point, he con-

tinued breaking down patterns into divisions and subdivisions, numbering 1,024 groups in all.

His accomplishment came to the attention of Scotland Yard,
and when the British Home Secretary in 1900 appointed a
commission to evaluate the subject, Henry was summoned to
explain his work. Pressed for a concrete example of what fingerprints might accomplish, he cited his successful solution of
a murder mystery in India. He had proved the guilt of a suspect
merely by establishing that the prisoner's finger mark on a
book was exactly similar to a print on the victim's body. His
account made a deep impression on the commission, which
was headed by Lord Belper.

On the commission's recommendation a fingerprint bureau
was created as a new department of the Yard, and in the
summer of 1901 Henry became its first director, a position he
held for nineteen years until he was succeeded by Frederick R.
Cherrill, still regarded as one of the greatest experts of all time
in the field. Of him it was said that one look at a fingerprint
gave him a mental picture of the person who had made it.

Almost from the start of his service Cherrill amazed his
colleagues with his almost uncanny ability to solve mysteries
using the clue provided by a single fingerprint or even a part of
one. He originated new procedures to simplify the work and to
add to its effectiveness.

Cherrill firmly supported the contention of his predecessors
that no two people had exactly similar finger marks. To an
earlier statement by Galton that the chance of an exception
was less than one in 64 million, Henry added that the possibility should be regarded as one in a septillion.

So far as is known at the time of writing, no two people with
matching fingerprints have ever been found, and much more
has been learned of nature's inexorable law of producing no
two things precisely alike. It is known that fingerprints appear
on a fetus after four months and remain without the slightest
variation until long after death. And if the patterns are marred
or obliterated by accident or through the wilfull efforts of
fugitives eager to conceal their identity, they return unchanged after healing has taken place.

That is why fingerprinting has been accepted by police de-
partments throughout the world, and in recent years it has
achieved notable results. In 1963 the ringleaders of England's

"Great Train Robbery" were captured through a mark on the wall of an abandoned farmhouse, and the assassin of the Reverend Martin Luther King was apprehended by a slender clue developed from a print on his rifle.

Such achievements were facilitated by a new development that took place in 1930, when Henry Battley, working in Scotland Yard, devised a method for separate filing of the prints of individual fingers as well as those of an entire hand. The "Battley Method," as it is called, is now in use almost universally.

While most courts in the United States and on the Continent were slow to accept fingerprint evidence, English jurists soon recognized its importance. In September 1902, only a year after Henry had assumed charge of the Scotland Yard bureau, legal history was made in London in the case of one Harry Jackson, who had been arrested on a charge of breaking into a house and stealing billiard balls. Jackson's plea of innocence collapsed when the men from the Yard produced the print of a right thumb found on a window sill and demonstrated to the magistrate that it matched the thumbprint of the accused.

Curiously, the acceptance of fingerprinting as a science in America was hastened by the imaginative story of a fiction writer, just as Conan Doyle's exploits of Sherlock Holmes had influenced advanced detective work in the days of Dr. Gross. Another powerful contributing factor was an extraordinary incident that took place in a federal penitentiary.

The fictional piece was written by Mark Twain in 1894, six years before the adoption of fingerprinting in England. Twain, who had read considerably of the work done by Herschel and Faulds, selected for his principal character an odd country lawyer popularly called "Pudd'nhead Wilson." The story was titled with the name of the writer's protagonist. As a hobby for which he was unfairly ridiculed, Wilson had been in the habit of inducing his friends to leave their finger marks on little strips of glass, which the lawyer carefully filed, identifying them with the names of those who had made the prints.

What Wilson's friends regarded as a stupid pastime suddenly won him wide acclaim. One day he found himself in court defending twin brothers accused of murdering a judge. Circumstances pointed strongly to their guilt, but Wilson won their acquittal by putting his hobby into legal use; he convinced the jury that the fingerprints of the accused were far different from those on a bloody knife found near the victim's body.

The story made a deep impact on the country, and the New York Police Department, nine years later, began fingerprinting all arrested persons. However, there were many who still scoffed at the idea. Their ridicule subsided some time later because of an incident in Leavenworth Prison in Kansas, an occurrence as weird as it was significant. It even rivaled the most fanciful imaginings of a gifted novelist.

One morning a tall, broad-shouldered prisoner was brought into the penitentiary. He gave his name as William West and asserted that he had never been in the place before.

"Oh yes, you have; I recognize you," snapped the identification officer, as he began taking body measurements in accord with the Bertillon system. The other was adamant, insisting that he had told the truth.

"No sense in your lying here," retorted the prison officer. "In a minute or two I'll prove that I'm right." With that he stepped to the telephone, calling a clerk for the file card on William West.

The record, quickly produced, bore a photograph and the usual physical description. The official carefully scrutinized the card, shifted his eyes to the new prisoner, and laughed. "Of course you've been here before," he said sarcastically. "This proves it."

There was a pause. "I admit that's my picture," the convict said with a puzzled look, "and you tell me that the measurements match but — believe me — I've never been here before. Somehow there must be a mistake."

"Okay, smart guy, come over here," the other ordered. "Let's get final proof — your fingerprints."

After West had pressed his fingers on an inked pad and made his marks on the usual form, the other man scanned them carefully, examined the patterns on the record card previously brought to him, and whistled softly.

"Say, these two sets of prints don't match; they're altogether different," he exclaimed. "I've never seen anything like this before."

For the first time the officer suspected that there might be another West in the prison. He took up the telephone again and in a short time a guard appeared with a convict in prison garb. "This here is William West," he announced. "He's been here for a while — doing life."

The two Wests, to all outward appearances as alike as two peas in a pod, stared at each other, too puzzled to speak. Despite their facial appearances and body measurements, their fingerprints failed to match. This case was widely publicized and attracted nationwide attention. The critics of Bertillon were jubilant. The certainty of fingerprint comparisons had been dramatically demonstrated.

Before long police in many localities initiated the fingerprinting system, which received still further support in New York through the astuteness of a detective named Faurot, who had gone to London by special permission to study fingerprinting and had returned only recently, eager to demonstrate what he had learned.

His opportunity came one afternoon when he chanced to visit the Waldorf Astoria Hotel on an official matter. On his way to the street he caught sight of a well-dressed man running barefoot down a dark hallway and looking furtively about him. The detective, his suspicions aroused, stopped the stranger for questioning. "I've been visiting a man's wife in his absence," was the quick explanation, and he vigorously protested his detention.

Faurot, however, took him to the station, where the man gave his name as James Jones, insisting that he was a well-to-do citizen of England, in the United States on business. The officer sent Jones's photograph and fingerprints to Scotland Yard, requesting a prompt reply. The New York police were soon advised that the prisoner was a notorious hotel burglar who had long been on the wanted list. On the following day he was aboard a steamer, heavily manacled, on his way to London.

Little more than a year later Faurot made a second significant demonstration. This time it was a murder case. The brutally beaten body of Nellie Quinn, a nurse, had been found in her room in a Manhattan lodging house. Faurot, closely scrutinizing the scene, found a lone print on a bottle and established that it was not that of the victim.

In questioning friends of the murdered woman, the detective's trail led to George Cramer, a plumber she had known.

His fingerprints were taken and one of them matched the mark on the bottle. Cramer confessed.

Despite these two cases and the West incident, American judges were reluctant to admit fingerprints as legal evidence until 1911. The change came during the trial of Thomas Jennings, accused of the murder of Clarence B. Hiller in his Chicago home in the fall of 1910.

Toward midnight Hiller had been awakened by the sounds of a burglar. Rushing into the hallway, he encountered the intruder and during a violent struggle the two rolled down the stairway. Moments later Mrs. Hiller, aroused by the scuffle, heard two shots and soon found her husband dead in a pool of blood at the foot of the staircase.

Jennings was arrested in the neighborhood a short time later by two off-duty patrolmen whose suspicions were aroused by his peculiar behavior, although at the time they knew nothing of the murder. They found a loaded revolver in his trousers pocket and took him to headquarters.

By this time the police had learned of the shooting and questioned their prisoner, but he denied all knowledge of the crime and explained an ugly wound on his hand by stating that he had fallen from a streetcar. A search of the Hiller home disclosed four fingerprints on the freshly painted ledge of a window through which an entrance had been made. They proved to be exactly similar to those of the prisoner taken immediately after his arrest.

This testimony, presented for the first time in an American court, became the basis of the prosecution's case. Jennings was found guilty and sentenced to death, but his lawyers challenged the validity of fingerprints as legal evidence. Late in 1911 the Illinois State Supreme Court upheld the conviction, and a precedent was set in American jurisprudence. From then on the new science was accepted by courts throughout the country, as it already had been in England and on the Continent.

As the taking of fingerprints by law enforcement agencies was spreading rapidly, it soon became apparent that some central body was needed to maintain and correlate records for the benefit of authorities everywhere. The Department of Justice then proposed to create such a bureau within Leavenworth Penitentiary and magnanimously appropriated "a sum not to exceed $60." The work was to be done by convicts.

The plan was doomed to fail. The prisoners were careless and frequently deliberately altered records for the benefit of friends. Bitter controversy followed, some believing that such a function should be under the Department of the Interior. The war of words continued until May 1924, when J. Edgar Hoover was appointed to head the Federal Bureau of Investigation and decided at once that all criminal records, including fingerprints, should be in his charge. That settled the question, since he was given full power to act. In a short time he began to assemble into one system all the records at Leavenworth together with those kept separately by the International Association of Chiefs of Police. This was the beginning of a massive collection of fantastic proportions, which now numbers millions of prints filed in the FBI's Washington headquarters.

Hundreds of volumes would be needed to list only the best known crime mysteries that have been solved in many countries by fingerprints alone. One of the most dramatic, illustrating the skills and perseverance of Scotland Yard, occurred in the summer of 1948 in the city of Blackburn, 210 miles northwest of London, and involved the kidnapping and murder of a three-year-old girl, June Anne Deveney.

Little June had been a patient at Queen's Park Hospital suffering from pneumonia but was recovering rapidly. A few days before her expected discharge she vanished from her hospital bed in the dead of night.

At 11:30 P.M. she had been observed by a nurse sleeping soundly beside five other children in the Babies' Ward. The nurse then stepped into a nearby kitchen to prepare food for the morning, and when she returned to the ward some twenty minutes later June's bed was empty. A door to the outside porch was open. Obviously the child had been abducted.

When a quick search of the building and surrounding grounds proved futile, Blackburn police were summoned, and in a short time the place was swarming with officers. Soon afterward the fiendishly beaten body of the little girl was found lying face up on a plot of grass close to a stone wall surrounding the hospital. Her head had been battered against the stones and she had been sexually abused. The killer apparently had left no clues.

Scotland Yard was notified and its chief superintendent,

Captain John Capstick, reached the scene a few hours later with a corps of men, assuming personal charge. He immediately ordered that no one be allowed to enter or leave the hospital.

His search of the place was well under way when a nurse called his attention to a large glass container called a Winchester bottle, which she had observed under the child's cot immediately after the disappearance was discovered. "It was not there when I last saw June," she said. "It was on the table with other bottles of the same kind."

Eager for fingerprints, Capstick picked it up with gloved hands and ordered that it be sent at once to the Yard. The only other discernible clues were impressions of bare feet close to the empty bed. The investigation was at its height when word reached Capstick that fresh prints of a left hand had been found on the Winchester bottle. They were to become the focal point of a worldwide manhunt.

Capstick, widely known for his meticulous attention to details, first compared the prints with those of everyone in the hospital, staff and patients alike. He then ordered the prints to be checked against hundreds of thousands of records at Scotland Yard. The results were negative.

For a month more than 2,000 suspects were rounded up and released, their fingerprints differing from those on the bottle. It was then that Capstick determined on a daring procedure — he decided to ask every male of Blackburn's 110,000 inhabitants to submit to fingerprinting. The mayor was the first to comply, and to spare the citizens from embarrassment, he arranged to have officers conduct a house to house visit to every man and boy in the city.

While this was in progress the search assumed worldwide proportions, with Scotland Yard tracing every serviceman and seaman who had left Blackburn within a period of years, and calling on police in faraway places to obtain the prints of the city's former residents. Weeks later Capstick reported that more than 48,000 prints had been received and checked; still the elusive killer remained at large. Circulars reproducing the marks on the bottle and detailing the nature of the crime had already been distributed to all parts of Great Britain, to continental countries, and to the United States. Capstick was particularly eager to have the prints checked with those of known sex deviates as well as with anyone who had been arrested for any type of crime.

Day after day disappointing reports reached Blackburn and Scotland Yard. Finally, in desperation, Capstick hit upon still another procedure, but he feared that if this also failed, there would be no further way to turn. He pinned his last hopes on fingerprint records taken in Blackburn of those who had received ration cards during the war.

The official in charge of these was instructed to send them, a few hundred at a time, to local headquarters to be compared with the clue from the bottle. The arduous task went on for weeks without results, and Capstick feared that the case would probably be listed as an unsolved mystery.

The break for which he had been hoping finally came early one morning close to three months after the hunt had begun. One of the experts was scanning one after another of the huge stack of ration cards on his desk. With a start, he suddenly detected a close similarity between the prints before him. He looked again, scarcely able to believe his eyes. Then he jumped excitedly to his feet, calling to his colleagues to verify his discovery.

The prints were those of Peter Griffiths of Blackburn, who had been in military service.

Capstick was quickly advised that the long search was over. With a squad of picked men he hastened to Griffiths' home, only to learn that he had left the day before with no word as to his return. A day and night watch was posted around the house, and for a time it was feared that he had escaped. Luck did not come until four days later when in the late afternoon one of the officers observed the young veteran walking leisurely toward his residence. Minutes later he was under arrest.

Young Griffiths stared at his captors with a look of surprise and inquired what he had done. Informed of the reason for his arrest, he insisted that he had not been near the hospital for years. He sat silently at the start of the drive to the station, then he suddenly blurted out, "Are my fingerprints why you came after me?"

Capstick nodded. "Then I might as well tell you all about it," he said meekly.

For an hour or more in the station house Capstick and his men listened to as sordid a story as they had ever heard. Griffiths readily admitted his guilt, recounting every detail of his movements on the fatal night, including the crime itself. He had been drinking heavily, he said, and had been driven by a friend to a point close to the hospital. What impelled him to enter he could not explain. He told of picking up the Winchester bottle on an impulse and quickly putting it down when he heard approaching footsteps. No one appeared, but little June began to cry, and, fearing detection, he picked her up and hurried outside. There her screams frightened him and he became a murderer.

He said he regretted the grief that could come to his parents but for himself he would ask no mercy. "I hope I get what I deserve," he told the officers after signing the confession.

Betrayed by the fingerprints he had left on the bottle, young Griffiths paid for his crime on the gallows.

Scotland Yard, however, is not alone in its long record of outstanding results achieved through the use of fingerprints. Files of America's FBI are replete with equally dramatic cases. They not only illustrate the successful use of the fingerprint technique in crime detection, but they also point out the criminal's fear of what the FBI can do with such evidence.

A case in point is the murder of two policemen whose bodies, riddled with bullets, were found in their patrol car parked close to a shopping center in Fredericksburg, Virginia. The time was early morning of May 5, 1964. Preliminary inquiry by the first detectives to reach the scene revealed that the murdered officers' handcuffs and revolvers were missing.

As the hunt for the slayers was being vigorously pressed, developments came three days afterward when police of Inkster, Michigan observed a car racing recklessly over a crowded highway. They called to the driver to halt but the demand was ignored, and the car continued on its way at an increased speed with the officers in hot pursuit. The chase ended only a few blocks away when the fugitive machine rammed a parked car whose driver was fatally injured.

The fugitive car driver was captured and identified as Walter Leikett. Two revolvers and handcuffs identical to those taken from the slain officers' car were in his possession.

When Leikett's fingerprints were studied by FBI experts in Washington, it was disclosed that he had a long record of car thefts and had been released from prison only a few days before on completion of a sentence for murder.

The FBI experts, however, uncovered still more. They reported that palmprints on the car in Virginia matched perfectly with those of the suspect Leikett.

Insisting on his innocence, the prisoner pleaded not guilty when he faced the court but the jury was deeply impressed by the testimony of the FBI men.

Leikett was found guilty by the jury which recommended a death sentence. An appeal was taken on technical grounds but when relatives of the convicted man reminded him that again he would be confronted by the testimony of the FBI experts, he changed his mind and entered a plea of guilty. This time he was sentenced to two consecutive terms of life imprisonment with the proviso that he would not be eligible for parole until he had been imprisoned for thirty years.

Once more fingerprint testimony had achieved its purpose.

Chapter 6

Hair Can Talk

I N JULY 1899 what came to be known as "L'affaire Gouffe" gripped the city of Lyon and many other parts of France. The reason was the baffling disappearance of a popular court bailiff in Lyon named Gouffe, a forty-two-year-old widower with a flair for women.

The mystery, after a long and vigorous hunt, was finally solved through the help of a few human hairs adhering to a brush belonging to the missing man. Significantly, it marked probably the first recorded effective use of hair by criminalists in the crime laboratory, and it led to other sensational cases being solved by the same means — cases in which hair was added to glass, dirt, metal, and other substances providing useful clues in crime mysteries.

When an intensive search for Gouffe failed to produce a single worthwhile clue, foul play was feared and the hunt for a body began. Many believed that he had been killed either through some emnity connected with his courtroom work or because of his private life. The investigation continued fruitlessly for four months, during which the press took the police seriously to task, contending that intelligent work would have brought about a solution. This criticism angered François Goron, then head of the French Sûreté, and induced him to take vigorous action. Assuming personal charge of the case, he called on his men in all parts of France to join in the hunt for the missing bailiff, dead or alive.

Some weeks had passed when a road mender in Lyon, walking through the woods on his way to work, came upon a badly decomposed body hidden in some shrubbery. There were definite signs of strangling but nothing by which the remains could be identified. Some suspected that the body might be that of Gouffe since height, weight, and other physical charac-

Francois Goron

teristics matched fairly well. Some were positive that it was not.

Relatives of Gouffe, summoned to view the remains, insisted that they were not those of the missing bailiff. Gouffe's hair, they asserted, was chestnut brown; the hair on the corpse was jet black. Thus hair color became the pivotal question in making a positive identification. Gouffe's long-time barber was sent for. He declared that though he had not seen his patron for some time, he did remember definitely that the bailiff's hair was chestnut brown.

Now convinced that the unidentified body was not that of Gouffe, detectives ordered the remains to be interred, but Goron hastened to Lyon and demanded that the grave be reopened and the body returned to the police laboratory. Goron stubbornly insisted that the difference in hair color, if it could be explained in some way, might well bring about a solution. But others scoffed at his belief in total disagreement and insisted that he was wasting his time.

Goron continued to stubbornly support his opinion, contending more insistently that hair might in some way prove to be a valuable laboratory tool. He claimed that criticism of his theory was prompted by an unsolved case years earlier in which attempts to use hair as a useful clue had failed. This mystery had resulted from the fatal stabbing of a Madame de Masel, a wealthy widow. When her body was found one hand was grasping three hairs, which investigators suspected she had pulled from the head of her slayer in a desperate struggle for life. Some had voiced doubt that the hairs were human, and since they appeared to be the only available clue, wigmakers from far and wide were called on for assistance, but no one was able to determine whether the hairs were human. At the time there was no scientific means of finding an answer, and the murder consequently remained unsolved.

In the following years biochemists and pathologists spent a considerable amount of time researching the entire subject of hair, convinced that by adequate study they could find a way of determining how to differentiate between human hair and the hair from lower animals. In fact, they were certain that by still wider study they could evolve a way of determining the value of hair as scientific evidence. Much progress was made, but as time passed no case arose in which the results of this intensive study could be put to use. "L'affaire Gouffe" apparently was the first.

While the unidentified body remained in the police laboratory, a battered old trunk was found close to where the body had been found. All efforts to link it with the unsolved bailiff case failed.

At this point a new idea flashed through Goron's mind. Still convinced that in some way hair would prove to be the key to a solution, he sent some men to Gouffe's apartment with orders to bring him the missing bailiff's hairbrush. It soon came under the scrutiny of laboratory technicians, who found five short hairs caught in the bristles. They were brown. Then hairs were clipped from the head of the unidentified corpse. They were definitely jet black.

Goron was still not satisfied. Suspecting for reasons of his own that Gouffe may have dyed his hair, he sent for three of the best known authorities in forensic medicine and asked for their help. These men subjected the hairs to new chemical tests that had been developed in recent years. Their conclusion was definite and unanimous — Gouffe had dyed his hair black. Now at least one phase of the mystery was cleared; no longer did anyone doubt that the body was that of the missing bailiff, who it was presumed had met his death at the hands of a strangler.

His remains were interred again with appropriate ceremonies, and many paid tribute to the court official who had been highly respected for many years. It now remained to find the killer or killers.

Facing this second phase of his task, Goron decided that the abandoned old trunk might prove useful as a clue. With the help of men from Scotland Yard and following many leads from a number of sources, Goron traced the trunk to London, where it had been purchased by a man in the company of a woman who later proved to have been his mistress.

Ascertaining their identity was a difficult and time-consuming task. Tracing their movements proved still more difficult, but detectives finally learned that they had traveled to New York together from France. From there they had fled to San Francisco, then to Canada, and finally to Cuba, where the two were arrested. By this time evidence had been unearthed linking the trunk and its new owners to Gouffe's death, which everyone now agreed was a case of murder.

The man eventually went to the guillotine, the woman to prison — both condemned by the silent testimony of a few hairs.

Of all the many cases in the United States and abroad in which hair has played a significant role as evidence, none is more dramatic than one that was solved by a pioneer criminalist of Berkeley, California, Edward Oscar Heinrich, who during a long and busy career utilized all the natural sciences in solving many mysterious criminal and civil cases.

In 1923 Heinrich was called on to assist the authorities trying to solve the daring holdup of a crowded Southern Pacific passenger train in a dark tunnel near the southern border of Oregon. Four men were murdered in the incident.

The holdup had occurred on October 11, 1923 in broad daylight, leaving few tangible clues for detectives to follow. But one clue, some believed, lay in a pair of dirty, well-worn overalls found on a bank near the entrance to the tunnel — a garment no doubt abandoned by the holdup men.

After a roundup of suspects had failed, the authorities turned to Heinrich for help, as they had many times before with effective results. One of his first moves was to take the overalls to his laboratory, explaining as he often did that at least a day was required to thoroughly examine any garment. Less than a week later he sent a note to the investigators stating that the overalls had been worn by a left-handed lumberjack, twenty-one to twenty-five years of age, a Caucasian with light brown hair, who had worked in the Pacific Northwest felling fir trees.

Detectives listened to the report with raised eyebrows, wondering how the Berkeley criminalist could have learned so much from a pair of jumpers. They had many questions to ask when they met Heinrich a few days later, all of which Heinrich answered to their satisfaction.

One of their major concerns was the expert's ability to tell both the hair color of the owner of the overalls and the fact that he was a Caucasian. Heinrich's explanation disclosed that he had done considerable research of his own and had absorbed all that had been learned in earlier years on the subject of hair as evidence.

He informed his inquirers that he had found a single hair

adhering to a button of the overalls.

"Now that you know how and where I found the hair," Heinrich continued, "let me explain what it told me when I examined a cross-section of it under the microscope. As you may know, hair can really be made to talk. The essential requirement is an ability to interpret what it can tell you.

"We already know," he went on, "that a Negro's hair is elliptical and that an Indian's hair is coarse and straight. We also have charts that disclose the structure of hair at various ages. That's how I was able to approximate the man's age. Any further questions?"

Heinrich had still more important information, however, which he had not included in his initial written report. Using a long, thin instrument of his own design, he had probed a narrow pocket on the bib of the overalls. It yielded a crumpled post office receipt for $50.00 made out in the name of Roy D'Autremont of Eugene, Oregon, payable to Ray D'Autremont in New Mexico.

Realizing the value of this lead, investigators asked for the help of post office inspectors and hastened to Eugene, where they located Paul D'Autremont, the aged father of the two named in the postal receipt. He admitted being worried about his three boys — Ray, Roy, and Hugh — who, he said, had suddenly dropped from sight on the same day as the train holdup.

Now the authorities were positive that the three D'Autremont brothers were responsible for the train robbery and murders, but they also realized that more clinching evidence was needed to link them with the crime. If they were captured and brought to trial the prosecution would certainly require an airtight case.

A bulky package of effects belonging to the three sons was taken from their father's home and sent to Heinrich. In the assortment of used clothing and other personal effects was a soiled face towel that the father said had been used by his son Roy. When Heinrich received the parcel at his Berkeley laboratory, he began a minute microscopic examination of its contents, including the towel that previously had been identified as belonging to Roy.

Heinrich's keen eyes soon observed a single hair adhering to the towel. Subjecting the lone strand to thorough examination and analysis, he concluded beyond the slightest doubt that it matched in every respect the hair found earlier on the overalls. Now, through the telltale testimony of hair, the authorities were convinced that the three D'Autremont brothers were the men they wanted.

Immediately a manhunt of history-making proportions was begun that set a new record for its thoroughness and far-reaching potential. More than two million circulars were printed in several languages and circulated throughout the United States, Europe, Asia, and South America. Liberal rewards were offered for helpful information leading to the capture of the trio. Months passed as hundreds of clues were followed without result. Numerous suspects were jailed, only to be freed when it became obvious that mistakes had been made.

Three years later Hugh was arrested in Manila, months after he had enlisted in the United States Army. He had been recognized by a fellow trooper who chanced to see one of the circulars on the wall of a post office. Though he denied his guilt after admitting his identity, the investigators felt certain that their manhunt was destined to succeed, though it might require more time. Hugh's capture obviously stirred the pursuers to still more determined and relentless efforts.

The hunt for the two fugitive brothers, however, might have continued for many years or perhaps ended in failure but for a stroke of sheer luck — an unexpected incident that would do credit to the imaginative mind of a fiction writer.

It occurred on April 13, 1927 in Steubenville, Ohio, many miles from the scene of the train robbery, where an aged man with impaired vision, Albert Cullingworth, was reading a newspaper account of the holdup and the long hunt for the three brothers. Fascinated, he looked at their pictures on the opposite page and a startling thought flashed through his mind.

"Two of these men look like the Goodwin twins working out there with me at the mill," he said to himself, peering again at the page through a magnifying glass. Cullingworth had seen them many times since he was employed at the same plant. A second look at the paper assured him that he was not mistaken. Wondering what course to follow, he finally thought of a woman he knew, a Mrs. Maynard, who ran a detective agency. Moving fast, he confided his suspicions to her and she, in turn, notified the FBI.

The "Goodwin twins" were soon arrested and admitted their identity, but news of their capture was withheld from Hugh whose trial was about to start in Oregon. The long manhunt was over.

Taken to Oregon for trial, they subsequently made complete confessions hoping to save themselves from the gallows. Eventually they were sentenced to life imprisonment in the Oregon State Penitentiary.

Two hairs, one on a pair of abandoned overalls in California and the other on a used towel in Oregon, had led to the capture and confessions of the three elusive train robbers. Science had triumphed again in the war against crime, and a new scientific laboratory tool had been added to those already in use.

Through the years hair has continued to play a dramatic role in scientific crime detection. In one case, a tragedy which occurred forty years after the D'Autremont affair, a single blond hair from an eyebrow brought about the solution of a baffling mystery and the capture of the culprit.

The case had its beginning in Houston, the largest city in Texas, early on a quiet Sunday morning, October 30, 1963. The scene was the parking lot outside a well-patronized bar, Holly's Lounge, where the battered body of a well-dressed man was found by a couple on their way to church. Close to the dead man's right arm lay an empty billfold and car keys. Papers on the body led to its identification as that of Orval F. Crain, aged fifty-four, a well-known and popular buyer for a wholesale drygoods company.

At first detectives theorized that Crain may have been the victim of a fist fight, for his face was badly cut and both his eyes were blackened. However, on second thought, the officers discarded this belief after being told that Crain was a mild, soft-spoken individual.

Sometime later, when closer examination revealed tire marks across the victim's white shirt front, the investigators suspected that Crain probably had been the victim of a hit and run accident or even of deliberate murder, with the killer purposely running his car over the body to confuse the police.

Inquiry among the Saturday night patrons of the bar added new mystery to the case. They said that Crain, who ordinarily mingled with the regular customers, had spent most of the evening conversing with a stranger, a tall man who did not "talk like a Texan." Search for this man proved futile.

Meanwhile police experts had taken plaster casts of tire marks in the parking lot. Comparing these with the markings on Crain's shirt, they concluded that he had been run over, dead or alive, by a light .weight pick-up truck.

Search for such a vehicle ended a few days later when a truck of such description was found a few miles out of the city. It had crashed into a telephone pole and been abandoned. A check of its license number showed that it had come from Oklahoma City.

Police examined every inch of the machine but could find nothing that could be considered a clue. A second check of the car was ordered and the task was assigned to Floyd McDonald, a crime laboratory expert, known for his almost uncanny ability to discover evidence where others had failed.

McDonald first ordered the truck moved to a garage. There, donning overalls, he raised it and crawled underneath, determined to scrutinize every speck of grime encrusted there and on the tires. Hours of tedious work passed until suddenly McDonald, thrusting an arm out from under the truck, called to his comrades excitedly.

"I think I've got something," he exclaimed excitedly, holding up in his fingers what later proved to be a slender blond hair from an eyebrow. He also had found evidence of dried blood.

In the laboratory the tiny hair was subjected first to tests which proved that it had come from a human body. Other tests established that it had come from Crain's, for hair samples had been carefully clipped from the body and preserved in case they should become useful.

The car eventually was traced to the dealer in Oklahoma City. His records showed that he had sold it to two men whose names he gave to the police. They were eventually located and one of them, John Crump, proved to be the tall stranger with whom Crain had spent time in the Texas bar.

When Crump was finally located and questioned, he admitted having been Crain's companion. The evening, he said, had ended in a fist fight in which Crain fell to the ground. Crump, in trying for a quick get-away, had backed his truck and accidentally driven over the prostrate form of Crain.

Technicalities interfered with Crump's extradition to

Texas, but when it was learned that he had been convicted of a felony some months before, he was sentenced to the penitentiary.

Chapter 7

Bullets as Witnesses

BULLETS CAN BE MADE TO TALK, but they need skilled inter-
preters. They can establish the guilt of the accused or they
can exonerate the innocent. Today they are doing both in
police laboratories throughout the world.

When the source of a bullet becomes of paramount importance, its markings must be compared with the grooves and
ridges inside the barrel of the suspected firearm or with a test
bullet fired from the same weapon. The barrel markings are
known as riflings, and if they correspond exactly with those on
the original lead pellet, the source of the bullet has been proved
beyond doubt. Rifling tools leave peculiar identifying marks —
tiny and usually invisible to the naked eye. These distinguishing scars make microscopic comparisons trustworthy.

The comparison technique is often erroneously referred to
as ballistics, which, correctly speaking, is the science relating
to the motion, direction, and general behavior of fired bullets.
Identifying weapons by rifling comparisons is properly called
"firearms examination." But experts often turn to ballistics to
determine, for example, whether a bullet has been fired by a
murderer or a suicide.

In modern practice, rifling marks within a gun barrel are
studied by firing a test bullet from the weapon into a bale of
cotton or a large slab of wax. In this way the bullet's markings
are not damaged, making possible an accurate comparison
with the original lead.

Interest in bullets and firearms for purposes of crime investigation began hundreds of years ago, according to Harry Soderman, who for years was head of the Institute of Police Science
at the University of Stockholm and who is still regarded as an
outstanding authority in criminalistics.

Soderman writes that the initial efforts centered on crude

*Two bullets fired from the same gun matched under a comparison
microscope*

attempts to match a bullet with the weapon from which it was fired. This, he explains, was a fairly simple process in the early days, because projectiles then were usually made by the individuals using them. As better and more complicated firearms, especially pistols and revolvers, were manufactured, new techniques for identifying their operation became necessary. Experts undertook to find a way. It was a long and difficult process; the answer came, as in other sciences, by progressive steps made by various specialists.

As early as 1740 a ballistic pendulum was developed, its purpose being to measure the velocity of a projectile. Consisting of a pendulum hung by wires to stop it swinging in one direction, it was first presented in about that year to the Royal Society of England by one Benjamin Robins.

Nearly a century later, in 1833, Henry Goddard, famed as the last of London's colorful Bow Street Runners (who preceded the London Metropolitan Police Force) made a noteworthy advance. Investigating a murder, he discovered a peculiar dent in a bullet extracted from the victim's body. In a suspect's home he uncovered a bullet mold of the kind then in use. Examining it closely, his keen eye perceived a flaw in the mold that corresponded precisely with the imperfect bullet. The suspect confessed and Goddard was widely acclaimed, though he probably did not envision at the time that he had laid the foundation for what would become a standard technique for tracing bullets to their source.

Some years afterward, after prolonged experiments, firearms manufacturers adopted a new and practical way of increasing the efficiency of their weapons. Tests had demonstrated that they could improve the accuracy and range of firearms by cutting spiraling grooves inside the barrels. They had reasoned that this was necessary because bullets, conical in shape, would turn end over end in the air unless they were put into rotation around a longitudinal axis through the pitch of grooves, which are known as "lands." They estimated that five or six grooves would be necessary — still the standard number today.

The improvement, however, was solely a matter of business as far as the gun makers were concerned. The better firearms they produced, the more they could sell. It remained for a skilled Frenchman, Professor Alexandre Lacassagne, to see in the new manufacturing process an opportunity for more effective crime detection, and he proceeded to introduce the process of comparing the marks on fired bullets with gun barrel ridges and indentations.

Despite Lacassagne's progress, there still remained a possibility of error: minute measurements could still be slightly inaccurate. But in the early 1920s another significant advance occurred, made possible by the cooperative effort of four specialists who each worked in somewhat different but related fields.

It was through the contributions of these four that the comparative microscope came into being. One of them was Charles E. Waite, a resident of New York. Appalled by the increasing number of homicides committed through the use of guns and by the widespread sale of firearms to criminals, Waite undertook to assemble from American manufacturers as many details as possible concerning the types of weapons, their modes of operation, their peculiarities, and the like. When he had completed this laborious self-imposed task in the United States, he went abroad to do the same. He gathered and classified an enormous amount of valuable information. He could look at a bullet and tell almost instantly from what type of weapon it had come, where and when the gun was manufactured, and by whom.

To put this great mass of data to worthwhile use, Waite needed to collaborate with others who were equally concerned. He found a colleague in John H. Fisher, a student of physics, who was working for the government. Then he met a forty-five-year-old American chemist, Howard Gravelle, a graduate of Columbia University, who had abandoned his interest in chemistry to devote his time to microscopes and photography. The fourth associate was a man from Baltimore, Calvin Goddard, who had become deeply interested in revolvers.

As a result of their joint efforts and the pooling of their specialized knowledge, the comparative microscope made its appearance, introduced by Howard Gravelle, and for the first time it became possible to compare, with unquestioned accuracy, a fired bullet with one ejected in testing a suspected revolver.

A few years later, the role of bullets and firearms in crime detection suddenly attracted worldwide attention in a murder mystery that became a cause célèbre in many countries — the case of two poor avowed anarchists, Sacco and Vanzetti.

Never before in modern criminal history had a crime in America created such worldwide concern, excitement, and violence. There were strikes, riots, bombings, and threats against citizens of the United States in many countries. Few civilized nations failed to join in the protests against the trial of the pair. Demands for their release came from marching crowds in Moscow, from the French and German governments, from South America and Australia. The accused men were praised as martyrs; Americans were condemned. Western democracy and its concepts of justice were put on trial, rather than the two Italians, and the issue remained alive for years. It even leads to heated discussion today, long after the execution of the pair on August 2, 1927.

While racial and political issues far transcended the strictly legal aspects of the case, attention was also focused on the controversial bullet and firearms elements of the evidence. Though the experts clashed, often with contradictory testimony, people everywhere came to realize that ballistics and firearms examination were now most important factors in the science of criminalistics.

The case occurred at a time when Americans looked with great dislike and suspicion on anarchist activities, which were led mostly by foreigners. There were angry demands that foreigners return to their own countries and that un-American utterances not be tolerated.

Against this background, the celebrated case is generally considered to have begun with an attempted holdup on the day before Christmas, 1919, in the town of Bridgewater close to Boston. There an angry group of foreign-looking men waylaid a truck carrying the payroll for a shoe company. Their demands for the money bags were met by a fusillade of shots from the guards aboard the payroll truck. The would-be robbers returned the fire, then fled and disappeared. The only clue was a discharged shotgun shell on the ground. The bandits could not be located and the authorities turned to other matters.

Less than four months later another holdup, far more serious than the first, occurred in the town of South Braintree, close to Bridgewater. In broad daylight two armed men attacked the paymaster of a nearby shoe factory as he was carrying more than $15,000 in a metal case with a guard walking at his side. Trigger-happy, they shot and mortally wounded both men, grabbed the money, and fled in a waiting car in which three men were seated. Baradelli, the guard, was dead before the ambulance arrived; his companion, Parmenter, succumbed some hours later.

While officers were hunting for the fugitive car, others began a search of the scene. It was soon apparent that bullets would be their most important clues. Four .32 caliber bullets were taken from Bardelli's body. Parmenter had been shot twice, though only one wound had caused his death. The six bullets were taken to the police laboratory together with four empty shells recovered from the pavement.

The manhunt had been in progress for two days when detectives located an abandoned car on the outskirts of town. It had been reported stolen two months before and resembled the vehicle used in the two holdups. The police apprehended two men who had been seen in the car some time before. They were Nicola Sacco, employed in a shoe factory, and Bartolomeo Vanzetti, who eked out a poor living pushing a fish cart. Italian emigrés, they spoke broken English. Literature in their pockets revealed them as active anarchists, but a complete search disclosed more damning evidence. In Sacco's pockets were a .32 caliber Colt revolver and bullets similar to those taken from the bodies of the dead men. Vanzetti was armed with a .38 caliber revolver.

The prisoners were soon identified by witnesses to the South Braintree murders, and their joint trial for the killings was set for the end of May 1921 in Dedham. No one doubted that bullets and revolvers would play a vital part in the state's determination to convict. That phase of the trial fell to Captain Proctor, head of the Massachusetts State Police, an experienced student of ballistics.

The trial had not progressed far when Proctor became the state's star witness, exhibiting the bullets and shells to the jury together with Sacco's revolver. At great length he related how he had fired test bullets from the weapon and compared them with the shot that had killed the guard. His final conclusion was that Sacco's gun had fired the fatal bullet. To further support his opinion, he testified that this bullet had left-hand spiral rifling marks, a distinguishing feature of the Colt — the make of Sacco's gun. Similar testimony was given by two other experts for the prosecution.

Their testimony was bitterly attacked by the defense specialists, and there were frequent clashes between opposing counsel. In the end the jury took the word of Proctor and his colleagues. Both defendants were convicted — Sacco as the actual killer, Vanzetti as an accessory. Death in the electric chair was their sentence.

At once the hue and cry provoked by their arrest and trial intensified. There were more riots, more protest meetings, and demands for a retrial. Books were written picturing Sacco and Vanzetti as innocent men; others took the opposite view, but in the end despite all the appeals and demonstrations the two condemned men paid with their lives.

The widespread feelings among so many in behalf of the defendants was based on two elements. Many believed that they had not received a fair trial; others contended that their conviction was due only to common hatred of anarchists.

Forty years later the issue, characterized by one writer as "the unfinished case," was revived in a magazine article portraying the two men as innocents. This led to a kind of posthumous retrial in which two widely recognized experts, one from West Point and another from the New Jersey State Police Laboratory, were asked to recheck the findings of the earlier experts. Using Sacco's Colt, they repeated the experiments that had been made nearly half a century before and concluded that the lethal bullet had been fired from Sacco's revolver. In any event, the world came to know that bullets could be material witnesses.

One of the strangest and most dramatic cases illustrating how intelligent study of a bullet and a revolver can lead to complete exoneration of a supposed murderer, even after his confession, took place in Bridgeport, Connecticut early in 1924. The hero of this extraordinary tragedy was Homer F. Cummings, then State's attorney for Fairfield County and later United States Attorney General in the administration of President Franklin D. Roosevelt.

The case began on the night of February 9, when one of Bridgeport's most beloved Catholic priests, Father Dubert Dahme, was shot and killed on a busy downtown street corner while taking his customary evening walk. It was a crime wholly without reason, for the priest was revered by the entire community, had no known enemies, and had never been involved in any controversy. It was presumed that he had been a victim of a religious fanatic who had set out to kill the first man of the cloth he encountered.

Witnesses to the killing and the murderer's hurried flight described the assassin as a young man of medium build, dressed in a three-quarter-length brown overcoat with a velvet collar. They related that they had seen him approaching the priest from behind with a black revolver in his hand. An instant later, the stranger quickened his pace, held the gun close to his victim's head, and fired. Father Dahme reeled, then fell forward. He died an hour later in the hospital.

In less than an hour every patrolman in Bridgeport had been alerted. Roadblocks were set up, and in many places cars were halted and their occupants questioned. By teletype and radio, police in every city and town throughout the state were instructed to be on the lookout for the killer. Here and there suspects were being picked up, only to be freed after satisfying officers that they were not involved. The wanted man had apparently vanished as suddenly as he had come.

Not until three weeks later did the statewide search begin to show results. In the city of Norwalk, close to Bridgeport, a policeman intercepted a young man standing on a street corner. His physical description and clothing fitted the wanted man, and though he denied any knowledge of the murder, he was hustled off to jail and soon transferred to Bridgeport. A loaded revolver with one discharged shell found in his possession added to the suspicions of the police.

The suspect said that his name was Harold Israel, that recently he had been discharged from the army, and that he had been trying to thumb a ride to his father's home in Pennsylvania. Asked about the weapon, he explained that he had been target practicing with three friends, but he was evasive when asked why he was still carrying it.

Witnesses to the shooting were summoned to the jail. Most of them said they recognized Israel as the gunman they had observed fleeing from the scene, though several appeared to be in doubt. Hours later a new witness appeared, a waitress named Nellie Trafton, who said that she had first met Israel while she was working at a lunch counter in the building where he had formerly lived. Weeks afterward she had accepted a new job in a similar type of restaurant less than a block from the scene of the murder. She was certain that she had seen him walking by that eating place minutes before the shooting, headed in the direction of the crime. Her statements became even more incriminating when she asserted that on one occasion Israel had shown her a revolver, stating that he intended to kill someone.

By now detectives were convinced that Israel was the assassin, and they pressed hard for a confession. Their questioning continued into the following day, but the prisoner did not waver in his denial of guilt nor could he be trapped into making any contradictions. His interrogators were relentless, alternating in pairs, certain that by uninterrupted pressure they could "break him down." It was a good surmise, for as the long afternoon wore on Israel gradually began showing signs of extreme nervousness and irritation.

The officers were quick to recognize the change and to press their advantage by still more vigorous questioning. Israel, perspiring, finally reached the breaking point. His face twitched and he wrung his hands. Then suddenly he jumped to his feet exclaiming, "I can't take it any longer. Yes, I shot him!"

A stenographer was called and Israel dictated a long statement, detailing the crime. "What did you do with the empty shell from your gun?" he was asked. He said he had left it on a shelf in the bathroom of his former lodgings. He was taken to the street corner where the murder had occurred, and his reconstruction of the crime fitted perfectly with the account given by the eyewitnesses.

The police, now positive that they had the murderer in custody, moved rapidly to complete their case. A firearms expert was summoned from Boston and instructed to make a laboratory study of the evidence. After studying the bullet taken from Father Dahme's body and Israel's revolver, he declared that the prisoner's gun had fired the fatal shot. This appeared to be the last link in forging the state's case, and Cummings, as State attorney, was told that he might proceed with the trial.

Cummings, however, was not so certain. After studying the evidence he grew skeptical, although he could not fully explain why. "There's something about this case that puzzles me," he told the police. "I can't exactly tell you what it is. Shall we say that it all looks too perfect?"

Long familiar with methods of crime detection as well as with the law, he determined to delve fully into the crime himself without outside help. Often he had been heard to say that a prosecutor's responsibility was not only to punish the guilty but also to protect the innocent. Despite ridicule from some police sources, he decided to start at the beginning and investigate every angle of the case. First he spent hours alone at the scene; then he interviewed the witnesses and of course the defendant.

Suspicious of the manner in which the confession had been obtained, he called on three highly respected psychiatrists to examine Israel. They were still at work when the prisoner unexpectedly repudiated his confession and asserted his innocence, explaining that he had been unable to endure the long and harassing questioning and that he had admitted guilt simply to end it. The doctors' report in essence confirmed his statement. They found Israel to be of low mentality, susceptible to suggestion, and unable to withstand long grilling. They also pointed out that his confession had disclosed no details not already known.

This was sufficient to convince the State attorney that he was not wasting his time. He decided to turn to science — the bullet, he knew, was the pivotal evidence. Had it really come from Israel's gun? Could the police expert possibly have been in error?

To satisfy himself he called on six of the most reputable and experienced experts he could find. He gave them Israel's revolver, the lethal bullet, and the discharged shells and told them to go to work, admitting that his judgment would rest on their final decision. He was not content, however, to remain idle while they were in the laboratory. Still working alone he interviewed the eyewitnesses and found glaring discrepancies in their accounts. One of them had insisted that the murder gun was black. Actually, it was nickel-plated, and when the lawyer took it to the murder scene at exactly the same hour of the crime, it glistened.

The experts' report was staggering. Following established procedure, they had fired test bullets from Israel's gun into a bale of cotton and compared the markings under the microscope with those on the lethal bullet. Their conclusion was that the shot that had killed Father Dahme had not come from Israel's revolver; the telltale markings definitely did not correspond in any essential detail.

Cummings carefully interrogated the men who had made the tests. "Can you explain," he asked, "the difference between the findings of the man working for the police and your own?" The answer was simple — the first man had not been conclusive in his report; he had merely said that certain markings had a "similar appearance."

Now Cummings was completely satisfied at last that an innocent man had been wrongly accused; a single bullet had spoken the vindicating words. However, experienced lawyer that he was, he wished to close every loophole before asking the court to free the prisoner. Since he was himself thoroughly knowledgeable in the field of firearms, he undertook to look for the empty shell that Israel had told of discarding in the bathroom of his former lodgings. When he visited the place, Cummings found not one but two shells. They had been discharged, he found, by a very dull trigger point although the trigger point of Israel's gun was unusually sharp, having been made so recently by a gunsmith.

Only two factors still remained to be clarified. One was the waitress, and when Cummings visited her place of employment and stood precisely where she said she had been when she observed the defendant, he realized that it would have been physically impossible for her to recognize anyone because of the considerable amount of lettering on the front window.

The last factor to be checked was Israel's alibi. He had insisted that he was in a motion picture theater at the time of the shooting. This, Cummings knew, should be a simple matter to verify. He called on Israel, impressed on him the importance of this final questioning, and demanded to know the exact titles of the films he had seen. These Israel easily recalled, and their sequence matched the theater proprietor's records. The lawyer's investigation was ended.

A few days later, on May 27, 1942, Cummings walked into the courtroom of Judge L. P. Waldo Marvin. He dropped a bulging suitcase on the counsel table and informed the court that he wished to read a lengthy statement. With the judge's permission he unfolded the entire story of his exhaustive investigation. The lethal bullet, of course, became the focal point of his presentation.

He read the report of the experts who had given him their conclusive opinion, then turned to the contradictory findings of the man engaged by the police. He had spent hours with this man, he said, while the latter attempted to superimpose a picture of the lethal bullet against a photograph of the pellet fired from Israel's gun.

"This man had great difficulty in getting them to coincide," the lawyer said. "In no way could I agree with his conclusions."

At the close of his extended remarks Cummings formally moved for a dismissal of the murder charge.

Judge Marvin slowly adjusted his spectacles and moved his chair forward before speaking. "The attitude of the State attorney's office," he began, "has been what it should be — one of impartiality and a desire to shield the innocent as well as a determination to prosecute those who are guilty." He proceeded to review the evidence, especially the exhaustive bullet tests, and again lauded Cummings for his meticulous efforts to learn the truth.

"I feel," he concluded, "that the State attorney's office is entirely justified in the recommendations that have been made and it is so ordered."

Israel walked out of the courtroom a free man. The murderer has never been apprehended, but an innocent man was spared from punishment.

A .32 caliber automatic pistol bullet, extracted by a pathologist from the body of a murdered eighteen-year-old girl, once served to send her killer to the penitentiary for life, with the unusual proviso by the judge that once each year on the anniversary of the crime he was to spend the day in solitary confinement.

The kidnapping and murder of Mary Ellen Lily Roberts occurred one balmy night, August 25, 1960, as she and her twenty-year-old fiancé, John Bryant Jr., a barber, sat in his parked car in a secluded lovers' lane near the famous Crab Orchard Wildlife Refuge in Williamson County, Illinois, planning their forthcoming marriage.

It was a serene, happy rendezvous until a strange car with

beaming headlights drove up beside them; moments later they heard a strange voice, obviously that of the man driving the other vehicle.

"Get out," the stranger commanded, and as young Bryant jumped nervously to the ground, a shot rang out and he felt a bullet enter his face. His wallet was taken from his trousers pocket. Then he heard the girl screaming his name in a cry for help, and he realized that she was being driven away by the bandit.

Bryant, despite his painful wound, succeeded in driving to a nearby highway where he was picked up in a semi-conscious condition and rushed to a hospital. His first thoughts were of his fiancée, and police quickly organized a thorough search, which later included airplanes and a helicopter. Bryant could only describe the bandit as a white man about six feet tall, wearing a white sports shirt and dark pants.

Roadblocks were set up but this measure, despite the help of hundreds of volunteers, failed to produce any trace of the wanted man. FBI agents joined in the hunt, and before long it had become one of the most intensive ever known in southern Illinois. The atrociousness of the crime aroused widespread public interest, which spurred the authorities to still greater action. Fears for the girl's safety were being felt, and many believed that she would not be found alive.

Meanwhile a search of the scene of the shooting had revealed a fired .32 caliber cartridge case, evidently discarded by the gunman, supporting the belief that the bullet fired at Bryant had passed through his face and lodged in the ground. This was their first clue.

As police looked hopefully for suspects among a number of questionable characters, they came to the name of Joseph H. Milani, who had been released only a short time before from the Illinois State Penitentiary after serving fourteen years for murdering a companion. He had also been in other serious trouble and was known as an irresponsible, dangerous man. Friends told detectives that he possessed an automobile similar in appearance to the car described by Bryant.

Milani's mother was contacted, but she insisted that her son was on his way to California. Further inquiry, however, disclosed that he had left town the morning after the shooting and returned the following day. Finally he was located, but despite intensive grilling he denied all knowledge of the crime, insisting that he had left home after a quarrel with his wife. Police decided to keep him under surveillance.

The futile search for the girl might have continued indefinitely but for a picnic held by a group of young people in a park some eighteen miles from the scene of the kidnapping. Roaming curiously about the place, one of the girls spied a well-filled water tank. Peering into it she detected what looked like soaked clothing. Moments later she saw a body. Police were called and the remains of the missing girl were recovered. She had been shot once in the head, and the bullet, it developed later, was of .32 caliber. Close to the water tank detectives found an empty cartridge case from which had been fired a bullet of similar size to that taken later from the girl's body.

Strong suspicion against Milani increased, and he was taken to the hospital where Bryant identified him as his assailant. Under severe questioning Milani admitted having purchased a .32 caliber revolver in a store in a nearby town a short time before, but he insisted that he had tossed the weapon into a river because he had no use for it and did not want it in his possession.

On the strength of the evidence already accumulated, Milani was indicted for murder, tried, and found guilty. He received the unusual sentence imposed by Judge C. Ross Reynolds, and he was taken to the state prison to remain there for the rest of his life.

As criminalists continued to utilize effectively their technique for linking a lethal bullet with the weapon that had fired it, they came to recognize the need for a way to identify accurately the person who had discharged the weapon. This would provide a vital means of pointing the finger of guilt without a doubt at a killer or at least an assailant.

Close study revealed that in most cases the person using the firearm sustained what are called "powder residues" on the hand holding the weapon. Close examination of these residues and the tiny almost invisible specks of powder adhering to the flesh became a technical and common way of determining the presence of combustion products from the fired cartridge on the shooter's hand. Admittedly, the method was subject to error.

What the criminalists needed was an exact, precise, and unquestionably reliable technique to reach a trustworthy decision. And this, despite the fact that for years powder particles, carefully removed with a paraffin cast from a hand and studied microscopically and chemically, had produced desired results. People were convicted or exonerated by use of this method but it finally remained for modern experts in the field to discover a means of making firearms discharge residues speak nothing but the absolute truth.

In the quest for what was required, electronics and ultra-modern electrical equipment were brought into play with results far exceeding the fondest hopes of those involved in this intensely complicated work.

A brilliant and exciting example of their present-day achievement can be found in the vast crime laboratory of the Sheriff's Department of Alameda County in California, a juris-diction sprawling for miles over the east side of San Francisco Bay. This laboratory, occupying the entire second floor of a spacious, rambling building in the busy little town of San Leandro, comprises numerous rooms crammed with micro-scopes and other technical equipment and almost defies description by lay observers. It has achieved nation-wide recognition as one of the foremost of its kind in the country, operating with ultra-modern electronic equipment and skills utilized in only a few other cities in America.

To this distinctive capital of science come forensic scien-tists from all parts of the United States. Advanced techniques and equipment have been utilized here for only a relatively short time, but many hope that the California experience will be emulated in many other sections of the country before too long.

Operated under Alameda County's Sheriff Glenn Dyer, the laboratory functions under the able direction of Robert M. Cooper and his senior criminalist, Tony Sprague. Both men, middle-aged, are highly skilled in their modern profession. Tall and serious faced, they might be taken to be college pro-fessors but for the long, white coats they wear at work. Both are university graduates and their ability to explain their work in simple, lay language would verify one's belief that they were teachers. They operate with a staff of seventeen skilled men and women.

Cordial, energetic, and enthusiastic, Cooper and Sprague state that their major purpose is to examine and interpret with utmost accuracy firearm primer residue — a task demanding the use of a highly complicated-looking machine known as a Scanning Electron Microscope which is coupled with an Energy Dispersive X-Ray Analyzer. At present, Cooper and Sprague assert, only a few other police laboratories in the country use similar equipment and procedures.

For the layman this microscope can best be pictured as a large console equipped with numerous knobs and dials. They describe the "heart" of the microscope as an electron column, a tall metal cylinder with a specimen chamber at its base.

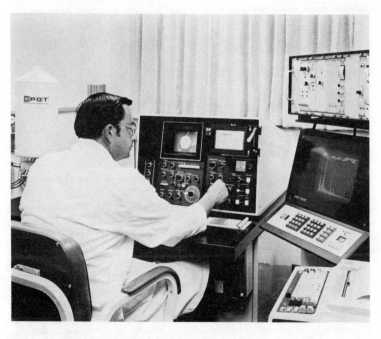

Tony Sprague at the console of the Scanning Electron Microscope

The device holding the gunshot primer residue particles to be examined minutely is fitted into the electron microscope. The device is a single disc about the size of a five-cent piece.

The gunshot particles or residue, Cooper and Sprague hasten to explain, come from the smoke and gases following the firearm discharge. Such particles can not be seen with the naked eye or even with an optical microscope. But with this modern analytical equipment the minutely-tiny specks under the Scanning Electron Microscope examination are enlarged many thousands of times — something that could not be done before. Under great magnification the unique form of the particles is revealed. It is then the function of the X-Ray Analyzer and Computer to interpret the elemental composition of each particle of residue recovered from a gunman's hand.

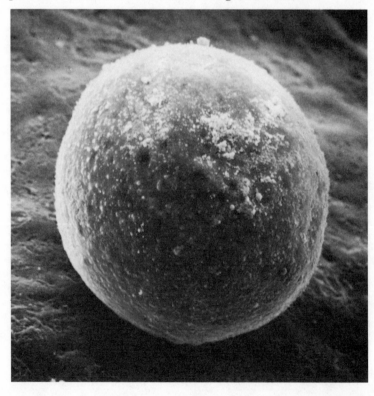

Gunshot residue particle magnified approximately 1050 times

Both laboratory experts are eager to relate cases in which their techniques and equipment have solved baffling firearm cases. They are quick to explain situations in which they have succeeded in determining that bullet-riddled bodies, first viewed as homicide victims, actually were those of suicides. In a recent case they successfully proved the guilt of a suspect who had fired recklessly into the front window of a home from a car parked outside, killing a lone resident.

People often ask how a police officer at the scene of a shooting can, without delay, accurately remove from a suspect's hands the residue of a fired weapon. Cooper and Sprague explain that gunshot residue collection kits, developed in the Alameda County Crime Laboratory, are used for the collection of this type of evidence. Specially trained crime scene investigators carry these kits to crime scenes where they may be immediately used. The kit contains sampling disks with implicit and illustrated instructions on how to proceed. In part they read:

> To collect gunshot residue from a person's hands the exposed tacky surface of the disc is pressed against the right hand until the disc loses its stickiness. Press straight down and lift straight up. . . .

> After the tacky surface has been used and the hand sampling is complete, the disc and plastic lid is firmly replaced in the glass vial from which it originated.

> Repeat these steps with the left hand.

And so, as emergency situations so often demand, every member of a law enforcement unit becomes a valuable adjunct to the ultra-modern work of today's crime laboratory.

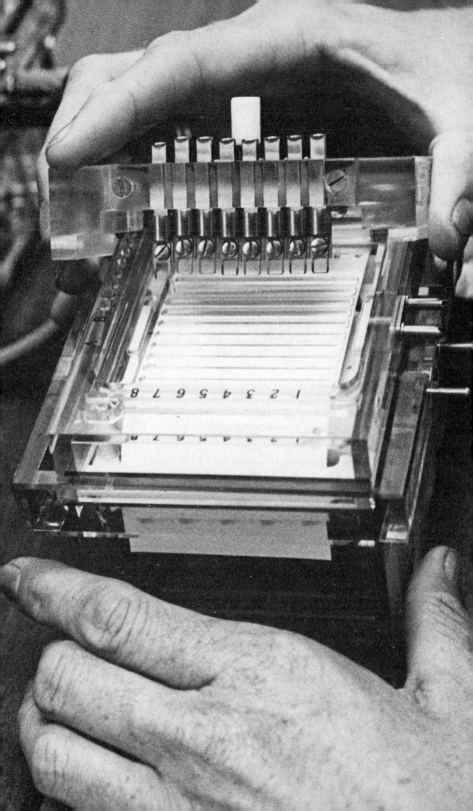

Chapter 8

Blood Reveals Secrets

U NLIKE HAIR AND FINGERPRINTS, blood was fairly slow in yielding its secrets for the benefit of criminal investigation. It was not until the turn of the twentieth century that serology — the science of blood, human body fluids, and serums — was fully accepted as an important field for laboratory research. One of the earliest problems confronting police authorities in this complicated field was how to detect blood stains, new and old, and how to distinguish them from other kinds of spots.

As with other forensic sciences, the names of the pioneer technicians are woven into the history of significant advances in the use of blood in criminal cases. Dr. Paul Jeserich, a Berlin chemist, was a pioneer in the middle of the nineteenth century. Others included Schönbein, also in Germany, and Van Deen in Holland. However, fully fifty years passed before the discovery of distinct blood types, long since accepted as basic in blood examinations.

Major credit for the earlier advances belongs to Jeserich. He began with the premise that although blood appears to be a simple liquid, it is in reality a body tissue with cells suspended in a fluid known as plasma, which makes up about 55 percent of blood. The cellular portion consists of red blood cells and a smaller number of white cells.

With a few colleagues Jeserich was endeavoring to improve the method of detecting bloodstains under the microscope by examining the shapes of the red cells, a procedure that was far from satisfactory. When the blood dried the cells would lose their shape, and to obtain microscopic results under such conditions it was necessary to apply a solution of alcohol and caustic potash to the suspected spots.

Fortunately for Jeserich but not for a certain murderer, an

Cellulose Acetate Membrane Electrophoresis — one of the most advanced blood analysis techniques (see p. 94) opportunity to test his technique developed in the midst of his work. This was a case of such sensational proportions that its denouement drew attention throughout Europe to the importance of blood as a major scientific clue. Jeserich was called on to establish whether the stains on a small wicker basket, long submerged in a river, were really bloodstains. His results were to mean prison or freedom for a man accused of murdering a little girl of nine.

The case, in all its dramatic and macabre details, is related by Jurgen Thorwald in his widely read book, *Crime and Science*, originally written in German.

The story began on the morning of June 11, 1904 with the finding of the badly mutilated torso of a little girl, wrapped in a bundle and bobbing up and down close to the shore of the River Spree in Berlin. The head and limbs were missing. Through a recent report of a missing child the police soon learned that the body was that of Lucie Berlin, a daughter of Frederich Berlin, a poor but hardworking cigar maker, who lived with his wife and two older girls in an apartment house in a run-down section of the city. Lucie had been missing for two days.

Who was the murderer, and how had the child been put to death? The police and all Berlin clamored for the answer. An intense search for sex deviates and suspicious vagrants in the neighborhood of the Berlins was under way when the coroner's report disclosed that the girl had been fiendishly violated either immediately before or soon after death. Public fury rose to new heights.

As detectives moved from one apartment to another in the shabby building housing the Berlins, interviewing residents in the hope of tracing Lucie's movements in the last hours before her death, they called at the room of a notorious prostitute, Johanna Liebstruth, who was celebrating her release from jail that morning. With her was a middle-aged man, Theodor Berger, her consort for some years, who sheepishly announced that they were soon to be married. They knew the murdered child well — she had often visited them — and in their excitement they told the police to look for a neighbor named Otto Lenz, who, they said, molested little girls.

Lenz was apprehended a day later, and though he admitted that he had sometimes played with Lucie, he insisted that he had no part in her death. It was obvious that the residents of the area disliked him, for they came forward to tell of his frequent walks with the victim. However, the suspect finally produced an acceptable alibi — he had been working in a remote part of the city at the time that the murder was supposed to have been committed.

As detectives turned to other directions for clues, interest began to focus on Berger, who appeared to be too eager to blame the other man. An inquiry disclosed many discrepancies in Berger's statements. It developed that for years he had been living on Johanna Liebstruth's illicit earnings and that he had a long prison record.

Police were centering their attention on Berger when they came upon their first tangible clue. A woman named Romer called at headquarters to report that on the day the body was found she had observed a man with a bulky, heavy package approaching the exact spot on the river bank where the grisly find was made. Her minute description tallied perfectly with that of Berger. She even mentioned a black dog she had seen trailing him, and police recalled that such a dog had been at Berger's feet when he was first interviewed.

With this information, detectives theorized that Berger probably killed the child in his apartment, dismembered the body there, and carried at least some parts to the water. In fact, they were so convinced of the soundness of their reasoning that they ordered the arrest of Berger and his female companion.

The two were on their way to jail when a small group of boys at play discovered Lucie's arms and legs floating in a waterway. Berger was taken to the morgue to view the remains. Though visibly shaken, he reasserted his innocence, even arguing that he was being detained unreasonably. The police, however, were now even more convinced of his guilt and decided to recheck his movements before and after the murder. While this was under way other police officers subjected Johanna to further grilling, and she unwittingly disclosed a clue that was to prove her paramour's guilt.

Bitter and resentful, she told the officers Berger had admitted to her that during her time in jail he had taken a strange prostitute to their apartment for the night and had given the woman Johanna's favorite wicker basket. His confession, she said, had led to a violent quarrel, and Berger had sought to assuage her with a promise of marriage.

The detectives exchanged curious glances, grasping at once the significance of the basket. Most likely, they reasoned, he had used it to dispose of parts of Lucie's body and been forced to invent an excuse for its disappearance. Berger in his cell winced when asked about it. He showed obvious signs of nervousness but still declared his innocence.

The river banks were searched in vain for the basket — a bitter disappointment to the police, who had hoped that the basket might still reveal bloodstains or other incriminating evidence. So it was proposed that Johanna's apartment be scrutinized a second time, and Jeserich, with an established reputation as an expert in blood clues, was asked to assist.

This was a wise move, for Jeserich had kept abreast of the work of a certain German chemist, Paul Uhlenhuth, who had succeeded in doing what earlier investigators in his field had found impossible — distinguishing human blood from that of animals. Time and again chemists called to the witness stand in criminal trials had been obliged to shrug their shoulders and admit reluctantly, "This spot is blood but we cannot tell whether it is from a human being or a lower animal. All I can say is that it is mammalian blood."

Now Uhlenhuth, after exhaustive and highly technical experiments with chickens and rabbits, had found a way of solving the problem. Prolonged tests proved the accuracy of his method.

In Berlin detectives stood by curiously as Jeserich, escorted to Johanna Liebstruth's dingy apartment, began his search. He examined everything — furniture, rugs, kitchen utensils, plumbing, and what remained of Berger's clothing. In one place where he observed a suspicious-looking stain, he ripped up an area of flooring; in another he tore off a strip of wallpaper. All this he carted away to his laboratory and set to work.

His results were disappointing. Despite his meticulous efforts, he could find no trace of blood. Frustrated, the police agreed that their last hope lay in finding the basket, but their renewed search was suddenly interrupted when a seaman walked into headquarters with the long-sought article. He had found it in the river days before, close to where the body had been picked up, but since he had not read the newspapers he knew nothing of the case. Carelessly he had tossed his find into a corner of his cellar. The officers were jubilant, though there was no certainty that this was in fact the basket they wanted. It contained only a hairpin, but wedged into a corner were scraps of paper similar to those around the torso. Further examination revealed a red spot that to the untrained eye looked like blood. An hour later Johanna identified the basket as hers.

Dr. Jeserich was sent for again, and in the presence of the anxious investigators he undertook to apply the Uhlenhuth test to the suspicious red stain. Before him stood three test tubes. Into one he dropped a reddish solution prepared from the basket stain. A solution from a clean piece of wicker went into the second vial; and the third he filled with a solution of human blood. Then to the contents of each test tube he added a serum of blood antibodies. In little more than a minute precipitation began to show in two of the vials — but not in the one containing a solution from the clean wicker. As the police had suspected, the basket was stained with human blood. The Uhlenhuth test had pointed a finger of guilt at the man in jail.

At Berger's trial the jury listened spellbound as Jeserich detailed the new process he had followed in determining the nature of the stain on the wicker. His method and conclusions were bitterly challenged by the defense but to no avail. Berger was found guilty and sentenced to fifteen years in prison. Johanna had already been released for lack of evidence.

The significance of the verdict far transcended the importance of the trial itself for a new milestone had been reached in the advancement of serology as a forensic science. No longer could those guilty of murder escape by pleading that bloodstains on their clothing had come from hunting or from killing fowls in their yards.

Fortunately for mankind, however, scientists are never still; they are not content to stop with one achievement; their eyes are ever set on new horizons. And so it was with the study of blood. Karl Landsteiner, a thirty-three-year-old assistant professor in pathology at the University of Vienna, was of that sort. With others in his field he had come to realize that there must be different types of human blood and that determining them would be an important step not only in medicine but in the police laboratory.

He was prompted by the many fatalities that followed attempts to transfuse fresh blood from healthy people into the bodies of the sick and aging. Working with such others as Theodor Billroth, a distinguished surgeon, and the physiologist Leonard Landois, Landsteiner had convinced himself that certain types of blood were not in harmony with others; that they did not mix. The scientists had established that red blood cells had a way of clumping, or to use the scientific term, "agglutinating." Why?

Landsteiner set to work to find the answer. He mixed blood cells with blood serum, a clear, yellowish, watery part of blood that separates from the clot when blood coagulates. Sometimes using his own blood and mixing it with that of his colleagues, he confirmed the fact that some blood was compatible with the blood of others and that some was not.

In the end he and his associates agreed that there were four master types of blood, which came to be recognized as Groups A, B, AB, and O. All human blood, they found, belonged to one of these four categories, distinguished by a chemical in red blood cells called agglutinogen. The A group has an A agglutinogen, the B group a B agglutinogen, and so on. The difference is easily established under the microscope, and among Caucasians, it was discovered, group O is the most common.

Putting this into practical use, if blood found on the clothing of a suspect proved to be of type O, it could not have come from the victim if the latter's blood belonged to type AB. Thus guilt or innocence could easily be established. In 1930 Landsteiner was awarded a Nobel prize in recognition of his achievement.

As time passed, other scientists went still further. The basic four groupings have since been subdivided into numerous others, their relationship understood only by skilled laboratory technicians. One of these is Margaret Pereira, who in 1963 developed techniques for the grouping of dried bloodstains. Another is Dr. Alexander S. Wiener of the New York City medical examiner's staff, a protégé of Dr. Landsteiner. With their help and the help of others many baffling crime mysteries have been solved through the years in the United States and Europe.

There are countless illustrations, none more dramatic perhaps than a case in the nation's capital a little more than three decades after Dr. Landsteiner had completed his historic studies.

The victim was an attractive forty-three-year-old woman,

Mrs. Florence Dougherty Goodwin, who supported herself by working as secretary to a Treasury Department official and by renting seven rooms in her large rambling old mansion on Sixteenth Street, in the center of Washington's Embassy Row. A divorcee, her marriage to a certain government official had been the subject of rumor for some time.

Of good family and with many friends, Mrs. Goodwin was extremely popular in her wide circle and often attended social functions. So the discovery of her murdered body in her second-floor bedroom came as a shock to many in the capital and as a challenge to the Washington police. She was found dead at eleven o'clock on a Friday morning, September 18, 1936, by one of her tenants, Mrs. Alphonse Billups, who with her husband occupied a room directly above that of Mrs. Goodwin.

The grim discovery might have been delayed for hours had not Mrs. Billups, with her instincts as a professional nurse, become worried on being told that Mrs. Goodwin, an early riser, was still asleep in her bedroom. Suspecting that her landlady was ill, she knocked repeatedly, and receiving no answer, opened the unlocked door and found the body lying on the couch in a pool of blood.

Recoiling from the room, Mrs. Billups telephoned the police and detectives were soon on the scene. It did not take them long to ascertain how the unfortunate woman had been killed. Her neck showed signs of a strangler's fingers and her head had been brutally battered with a blunt instrument. The bedroom, it was found, could be entered by either a front or a rear stairway through a kitchenette, but the doors leading to each staircase had been locked the night before.

The lack of any clue as to motive added to the mystery. Mrs. Goodwin had not been criminally attacked, and a search of her bedroom showed no signs of robbery. Only a twenty-five-cent piece was found in her purse but the room had not been disturbed. Books revealed that she had been a student of the occult and had delved into astrology. Here and there were loose papers on which she had scribbled verses.

Ira Keck, assistant chief of detectives, and Lieutenant John Fowler, the department's criminalist, assumed charge. Their first move was to look for the murder weapon and to question all the occupants of the house. It appeared from the start that the crime was "an inside job."

One of the first to receive their attention was Mrs. Goodwin's houseboy, Charles Chase, a twenty-five-year-old student at Howard University who was working his way through college. Mrs. Billups had met him just outside Mrs. Goodwin's bedroom shortly before she found the body. He was writing a note to inform his employer that he had finished his chores and was on his way to the laundry but would return.

"She's usually up long before this," remarked Mrs. Billups. "Why don't you knock on her door?"

Young Chase shook his head. "She's always warned me not to awaken her," he explained. "She probably wants to sleep late this morning." Mrs. Billups had thought otherwise and so became the first to find the body.

A minute search of the house revealed the lethal weapon hidden in an unused basement boiler. It was an iron stove lid about two feet long, weighing about ten pounds. That it was the deadly weapon there was no doubt, for one end was massed with blood, some still wet. The handle had been wiped clean, presumably to remove fingerprints. Stuck in the bloodied end were several hairs that Coroner A. Magruder MacDonald said matched perfectly with those of the victim.

The time of death was fixed by MacDonald at about six o'clock that morning. This checked with the word of a lodger who said he had heard his landlady moving about at approximately that time, though an hour later he had knocked on her door and received no response.

By this time all Mrs. Goodwin's lodgers had been brought to the house from their places of employment for questioning. None could offer any help, and the police, still believing that the crime had been committed by someone in the house, ordered all the tenants to be shadowed. Guards were posted to watch for any visitors.

Chase, the houseboy, was arrested though he proclaimed his innocence. He was asked to remove his clothing, and his trousers produced the first important lead — a tiny spot that looked like blood. His fingernails were carefully scraped under the direction of Dr. Oscar B. Hunter, a prominent pathologist, who found a second incriminating clue — two thin little strands of blue thread.

These Dr. Hunter took to his laboratory, and while he went to work with his microscope detectives undertook to check

Chase's alibi. He claimed that he had not reached the house until seven thirty that morning, and he gave the officers the names of friends who had seen him leave his own lodgings half an hour before. However, no one had been with him at six o'clock, the estimated time of the murder.

While Chase, despite his protests and avowed affection for his employer, was viewed as a logical suspect, the detectives also began to search for another man. They had learned from several of Mrs. Goodwin's lodgers that a certain John Thompson had been hired by her some months before as a janitor and had been suddenly discharged — no one knew why.

Locating Thompson, described as twenty-seven years of age and six feet tall, was not an easy matter. The telephone book listed numbers of men of the same name, but the police were determined to find him, more to eliminate him than to produce a new suspect; Chase was still regarded as the probable killer. Three days passed before the hunt came to a successful end. Thompson was arrested as he entered his home after an unexplained absence. A tip picked up in a poolroom had produced results.

At headquarters Thompson was searched, and the first thing to attract attention was a wide brown spot on his shirt. His fingerprints revealed that his true name was Norman Wesley Robinson and that he had served time in Pennsylvania and other states for robbery. Though he vigorously denied any connection with the murder, his shirt was sent to the laboratory and his fingernails were scraped. Like Chase's, they produced two slim threads of blue silk. If he had choked Mrs. Goodwin his nails must have come into contact with the silk dressing gown she was wearing at the time.

Now the police faced a real dilemma: they were holding two important suspects and the evidence against both was incriminating. Obviously, under the circumstances, the two could not have worked together. Thoroughly puzzled, the police looked anxiously to the laboratory for a solution.

Dr. Hunter's first report came in twenty-four hours. He had examined the frail silk threads taken from the nails of both prisoners and studied them under strong lenses. He had only one conclusion — in both cases the threads had come from Mrs. Goodwin's dressing gown.

It was difficult to interpret so confusing a report, but the detectives were inclined to believe that as far as Chase was concerned there was at least some plausible reason for the presence of threads under his fingernails. It had been his duty to make his employer's bed. In doing so, it seemed possible that his hands would come into contact with her clothing. No so, however, with Thompson, who now had been revealed as Robinson.

When this surmise was explained to Dr. Hunter he told the officers to be patient, that the answer they sought might come from the laboratory after he had completed his work with the bloodstains — the spot on Chase's trousers and the stain on Robinson's shirt.

"I don't need to tell you," he said, "that we are able to classify blood into four major types. In fact, we have numerous other classifications that distinguish the blood of one person from that of another. Why don't you reserve judgment until I've finished the last step in my examination — the blood."

They waited impatiently through an anxious day. It was early evening when a call came from Dr. Hunter. "I'm reasonably satisfied that you can release Chase, the houseboy," he announced.

"So soon!" exclaimed Lieutenant Fowler on the other end of the line. "What have you found?"

"Just this," the scientist replied. "The blood of Mrs. Goodwin and that on Chase's pants don't match. They are of different types."

"What about Robinson?" Fowler inquired.

"Now that's a different matter," said the man in the laboratory. "Mrs. Goodwin's blood is of a rare type and so is the blood on Robinson's shirt. They match perfectly in every respect. Have I said enough?"

He had indeed. The science of serology had provided the answer.

That night Fowler and Keck called Robinson from his cell, gave him a chair in the guarded conference room, and resumed their questioning. For a time the man parried their queries in a haughty manner, protesting his guilt and defying the officers to provide proof. First they showed him greatly enlarged photographs of the thin little shreds of silk taken from his fingernails. Robinson's answer was a forced smile.

This, however, was only a beginning. After a time they

exhibited large reproductions of the red corpuscles as seen through the microscope. "These are from the blood on your shirt," they told him, "and this picture shows they are exactly the same as those from Mrs. Goodwin's blood. One of the greatest pathologists in America says they are identical in type. Now what have you got to say?"

For some moments Robinson stared silently at the ceiling. Then he began to sway. His lips moved but no words came. Then suddenly he blurted out, "Yes, I killed her — no use denying it any longer."

An hour later he was at the Goodwin home reenacting the crime. Robbery had been his motive, he said, for he believed that she had money and jewels hidden about the house. On leaving her employment months before, he had taken the cellar key with him.

On the morning of the tragedy, he admitted, he had used it to enter the basement. There he had picked up the stove lid lifter and sneaked up the rear stairway to the woman's room. Listening for a moment and hearing no sound, he tiptoed in, picked up the almost empty purse, and began looking in the bureau. Then Mrs. Goodwin seemed to open her eyes and move. Stepping to the bedside, he struck her repeatedly over the head, and to make certain that she was dead he grabbed her throat and pressed until he heard her larynx snap.

Then he carried the death weapon into the cellar and threw it into the old boiler after carefully wiping the handle to remove his fingerprints. "I never imagined that the blood spot on my shirt could tell anything to the police," he said.

On March 18, 1938, after nine stays of execution, Robinson, then twenty-eight years of age, paid with his life in the electric chair in the district prison. Tragically, another milestone in the history of serology had been reached. The innocent Chase had been completely exonerated. He recalled having cut himself while shaving, which explained the little red spot on his trousers.

As one would expect, the need for advances in serology and its practical use in scientific crime detection have not been overlooked in Northern California's widely acclaimed laboratory, referred to in the previous chapter. Serology is the science that studies blood and its components.

In the Alameda County Crime Laboratory research and years of experimenting are in the hands of an attractive, tall young woman, Ms. Pat Zajac, a criminalistics graduate of the University of California's Criminology Department, in endeavoring to broaden the techniques of her intriguing field.

Stains of dried blood found on the bodies of victims and at the scenes of mysterious crimes reach her daily, and she spends hours peering into microscopes and using specialized equipment to separate genetic components of the blood, in order to determine precisely what these specimens of dried and fresh blood can be made to reveal.

Pat Zajac has progressed far in breaking down the established and commonly recognized types of blood. This she has achieved with internationally-recognized success.

Until recently, only the ABO blood group was determined in dried bloodstains. This crime laboratory now has the capability of determining as many as ten genetic systems in human blood, in addition to the traditional ABO, greatly increasing the statistical likelihood that a spot of dried blood could have come from a victim or suspect.

Using a technique called electrophoresis, which separates the component parts of the blood, Ms. Zajac identifies the numerous genetic markers — enzymes and proteins — from a tiny drop of dried blood. This technique of Cellulose Acetate Membrane Electrophoresis has superseded the older, cumbersome methods initially developed by the Metropolitan Police Laboratory in London (New Scotland Yard). The old methods using a starch gel were tedious and time-consuming and were not widely adopted in the United States. The methods developed by Ms. Zajac, in collaboration with a University of California Research Laboratory, provide for a more rapid, sensitive, economical, and reliable analysis of dried bloodstains. Analyses that required 25-30 hours by the old methods can now be done in less than an hour at the Alameda Crime Lab. Bloodstains even many years old yield valuable identification evidence.

She speaks interestingly of the many cases in which she has played a major role, cases that began as baffling mysteries but were finally solved completely by what she learned from bloodstains on bodies or clothing; or on such lethal weapons as knives, daggers or shotguns. In one case, two victims of a brutal murder and the suspect all shed blood and all had the same ABO blood group — Type O. It was only through the analysis of the enzyme and protein systems that the dozens of bloodstains at the scene, on clothing, and on the weapons were identified and determined from which person each stain could have come.

Enthusiastic over her success in establishing many new classifications for blood types, Ms. Zajac aspires to higher academic degrees in Forensic Science, as she labors diligently in the laboratory she has served since 1970.

Her observing eyes and deep knowledge of science have made blood talk to convict the guilty or exonerate the innocent.

Chapter 9

Reading Between the Lines

HANDWRITING EXPERTS, including the famous Albert Osborn of New York, agree that it is impossible for anyone to imitate another's writing perfectly. The habits of a lifetime, they contend, cannot be acquired in moments by a forger — however clever he or she may be. The distinguishing characteristics of the writer are always detectable to the trained eye of the professional investigator.

Paper and ink as evidence are often valuable aids to experts in this field, who now utilize many scientific means such as microscopes, ultraviolet rays, spectographs, and chemical tests.

Delving into history, experts have found that forgery is by no means a modern crime, although the genuineness of a signature, a line of script in a will, a business agreement, or a ransom note sent by a kidnapper still often plays a determining role in solving civil or criminal disputes.

The ancient Greeks, Assyrians, Romans, and Egyptians, according to the experts, were clever in forgery, and some inhabitants of Sparta, Athens, and Babylon learned how to bleach manuscripts in a way that would make forgery difficult or sometimes even impossible. The history of the early Christian era is replete with accounts of bitter and prolonged controversies over the authenticity of important documents and art works.

In the absence of the techniques and scientific tests used today in the comparison of handwriting, early offenders often escaped punishment. But in later years some who have expertise have been mistaken in their judgments. Men condemned as forgers have on occasion won final vindication through the efforts of those with adequate skills to establish the truth. Much credit now goes to men like Edward Heinrich, Osborn,

Luke May, and Hans Schneickert, the latter having been director of the Identification Bureau of the Berlin police until 1928.
Years earlier Hans Gross made a notable beginning in this
field.

While the general approach of the experts is usually the
same, some are inclined to place more emphasis on certain
characteristics than on others. Most of them pay special attention to word terminals — upward, horizontal, or downward —
and to connections. Today's experts, undertaking a complicated study, use their microscopes to examine every stroke of
the pen or pencil. In one case, described later in this chapter,
an examiner was even able to conclude that the writer was
handicapped by a stiffened right thumb.

On rare occasions experts are confronted by puzzling problems arising from the practice of using invisible writing
materials like milk, lemon juice, or saliva. It has been found,
however, that with proper scientific treatment and illumina-
tion such writing can be made legible.

Tracing can also become an important element. In some
instances forgers will trace a signature onto another piece of
paper; less frequently they will attempt to erase using ink
eradicators, rubber, or knives, but if the paper has been altered
erasures can be detected with little difficulty, usually with the
help of the ultraviolet ray.

This was once learned by an ingenuous burglar who believed
that he had conceived a foolproof scheme, which unfortunately for him failed to fool the experts.

This man, operating in the Pacific Northwest, broke into a
large building in which many dentists had their offices. The
burglar, after looting many of the dental offices of gold and
silver, escaped by airplane to a small town in the Midwest
hundreds of miles away. There he engaged a room in a cheap
lodging house and thoughtfully laid his plans.

He induced the desk clerk to leave on an errand, and, alone
in the office, the newcomer quickly scanned the register trying
to find a guest's name written on the same day as the burglary.
This was not difficult. Then, using an ink eradicator he had
brought with him for the purpose, he erased the name and
wrote in his own. Now he was convinced he would have an
airtight alibi in the event of capture to prove that at the time
of the crime he was in another state. However, he did not

anticipate the skill of the handwriting experts.

Some weeks later he was captured miles away on the basis of the hotel clerk's description and promptly asserted his alibi as proof of his innocence. Detectives went to the rooming house and examined the signature with trained eyes. A handwriting expert was summoned and he quickly discovered the deception. The burglar went to prison.

In the field of forgery detection, a humorous situation once developed to deflate the ego of a celebrated prisoner in San Quentin Penitentiary in California, a musician named Damasus Gallur, who was serving a life sentence for murder.

Gallur had gained nationwide attention by winning a large cash prize for an original composition commemorating the completion of the Panama Canal. It was a march that he had written while sitting alone in his prison cell, working in competition with many composers all over the country. Proud of his success, Gallur told reporters that he would continue to compose music in spite of his handicap, and months later he showed them checks for large amounts that he had received from music publishers in payment of royalties.

His achievements were reported in the press, but the denouement came some time later when inquisitive prison officials learned to their surprise that Gallur had been working with a clever forger in the prison who had accommodatingly raised the amounts of the royalty checks, so that a check for $1.20 became a check for $1,200. Kindly authorities never told him that his trickery had failed. Obviously they wanted to spare him chagrin. He had committed no crime, as he had not attempted to cash the checks.

Luke May liked to tell of a case in which he not only unmasked a forger but proved him to be a murderer.

This case involved a sudden turn in the life of an ex-convict, James E. Mahoney, who had been in trouble previously for assault. When Mahoney, never affluent, suddenly displayed a small fortune in diamonds, word reached the police and he was summoned for questioning. He had a quick explanation, stating that he had recently married a wealthy widow. The gems, he claimed, had been entrusted to him while his bride was on vacation in Cuba. They had traveled together as far as

St. Louis, he related, and parted there as his wife continued on her way with a woman friend.

Pressed for proof, Mahoney reached into his pocket and took out a love letter from his wife as well as a book of travelers checks bearing her name. He also displayed papers giving him power of attorney. But the police were far from satisfied. If they could not verify Mahoney's statements through his wife, they at least could question some of the couple's friends. In the meantime, they decided to detain Mahoney pending results.

It did not take detectives long to learn that their suspicions were well-founded. Mahoney, they discovered, had already sold some of his wife's real estate; moreover, friends asserted that she had always been in the habit of keeping her diamonds in her own possession. The genuineness of the power of attorney now came under suspicion. May was given the travelers checks together with examples of the woman's handwriting. It did not take him long to conclude that the letters and signatures displayed by Mahoney were definitely forged.

Now it became necessary to locate Mrs. Mahoney, and the Cuban authorities were called on for assistance. After several days had passed without any helpful information, detectives decided to inquire into Mahoney's movements on the day he said he had left home with his wife for St. Louis. To their surprise they learned that before his departure he had appeared before a notary public with a woman he introduced as his wife but whose description did not match that of his spouse; actually he was with his sister, a Mrs. Johnson.

Other developments followed in quick succession. From a trucker the investigators learned that he had carted a heavy trunk from Mahoney's apartment and driven it and Mahoney to a lake, where Mahoney had lifted it into a boat in which he rowed away. A storekeeper told the police that Mahoney had purchased rope and lime on the same day.

Months later, after an intensive search, the trunk was recovered in the muddy bed of the lake. In it was the crumpled and badly decomposed body of the missing woman. Mahoney was proved to be not only a forger but a killer as well. He paid with his life on the gallows, and his sister, convicted of forgery, was sent to prison.

One of the most bizarre cases illustrating the value of expertise in handwriting fills a bulky file in the archives of the United States Supreme Court in Washington. This is the case that revealed Edward Heinrich's extraordinary ability not only to establish forgery but also to ascertain that the suspect was handicapped by a stiffened thumb joint.

The case had its origin in the hectic days of the prohibition era, when rumrunning, bootlegging, and speakeasies were a part of the new American way of life. At great expense and with a small army of agents spread across the country, Uncle Sam was trying his utmost to stem the flow of contraband liquor from Canada and other countries into the United States.

Government officials were especially concerned at this time with the operations of a large Canadian freighter, the *Quadra*, which was defiantly bringing large Canadian shipments to California ports. Every effort to trap the vessel inside the twelve-mile limit of American waters had failed, but prohibition officials continued their efforts to capture the rumrunner.

The long-awaited encounter came on October 12, 1924, outside the Golden Gate, the entrance to San Francisco Bay. It ended days and nights of watchfulness by Lieutenant-Commander C. F. Howell of the U.S. coast guard cutter *Shawnee*, who had been playing a cat-and-mouse game, eager to catch the Canadian freighter in American waters. It was close to noon when Howell, peering through his binoculars, satisfied himself that the heavily laden vessel had sneaked into waters under American jurisdiction. Quickly steering his cutter in the *Quadra*'s direction, he approached at full speed and was soon close enough to speak to the other vessel and demand surrender.

His command was ignored by the *Quadra*'s skipper, Captain George Ford, who insisted that he was fourteen miles off shore, and for a time the two captains exchanged angry words, using megaphones. In the end Howell ordered three of his men to board the Canadian ship, which was to be towed into port as a prize. The coastguardsmen had barely begun their work with hawsers when they spied a small motorboat pulling away from the port side of the *Quadra*. Howell was signaled and when the little craft ignored his order to halt, the *Shawnee*'s skipper sent three shots over the heads of those in the boat. This brought quick surrender, and the craft, loaded with sacked liquors, was made fast to the cutter.

Both vessels were brought into port and their crews taken into custody. As had been expected, the *Quadra*'s holds and decks were filled with a fortune in Canadian liquors. Government men were carefully examining their evidence when they met with a surprise. An employee of the Federal Reserve Bank had walked into the office of the United States Secret Service with eighty-three one-dollar bills that had been exchanged at the bank. Handing them to Captain Thomas Foster, the local Secret Service chief, he pointed to a peculiar circumstance — all the bills had been torn in half and put together with tape. On the back of each were notations, some handwritten and some typewritten, enumerating specific amounts of different liquors.

"Do you know who left this currency at the bank?" Foster inquired.

The other nodded and gave the name of a prominent man who had long been suspected as the western representative of the northern rumrunners. To spare an innocent family he will be identified here only as Vincent Baraciola, which was not his real name.

Foster and the other federal investigators, working together since the beginning of the case, were still trying to unravel the mystery of the torn currency, when the answer came unexpectedly from a shabbily dressed boatman who had been arrested before the *Quadra* incident and had finally confessed to his insignificant part in the liquor smuggling. He explained that the torn bills provided a way of contact by which the captains of "mother ships" at sea could tell that launches calling for liquor to be brought ashore were really members of the ring. On the back of one half of a dollar bill was written or typed the exact amount of liquor to be delivered. This part of the currency the skipper would match with the other half given to him before leaving Canada. It was all very simple and apparently safe. But the federal investigators now had to identify the writer; so they sent for Heinrich.

He took the torn bills to his laboratory and examined the writing for days under the microscope. Then he called for the writing of several suspects, including Baraciola. A few days later he made a second request: "Get me a sample from Baraciola's typewriter."

This was a difficult assignment, but prohibition agents had

a way of getting the evidence they needed. After Heinrich had studied all the specimens he declared that beyond doubt the handwriting was that of Baraciola and the typed notations were the work of his machine. As was his custom, Heinrich was not content merely to report his findings; he always wanted to explain how he had reached them, and in this case he explained how the writer had held his pen.

"My study of the manner in which the writer operated his pen," Heinrich reported, "was based on the determination of points at which the pen nibs crossed and recrossed each other.

"This writer in all cases holds his pen in such a way that the angle of reference or the angle of the hollow of the pen to the baseline, is approximately forty degrees; the pen is held with the end pointing over the elbow away from the body, and it results in a form of writing that has a slope of approximately forty-five degrees."

This, however, was only one phase of the task assigned to Heinrich. The federal men sent him the *Quadra*'s log taken from the quarters of the supercargo, James McLellan. It was a puzzling book, filled with cryptic notations that appeared to chronicle the *Quadra*'s movements and transactions, telling where and when liquor shipments had been received and delivered. There were such entries as, "Picked up *Kilturah* and took aboard 204 sacks R. beer and 380 boxes. Discharged aboard *Kilturah* 3,374 cases." All the others were of a similar nature.

Their meaning was of course important, but their authorship was of still greater concern. If it could be shown that McLellan had made the entries, he could definitely be linked with the rumrunners' illicit traffic. So the log was turned over to Heinrich with known examples of the supercargo's handwriting.

In a few days the expert definitely confirmed the suspicions of the investigators; he reported that he was positive McLellan had made the entries in the log.

"Is this a certainty?" one of them inquired.

"Beyond a doubt," Heinrich answered with assurance. "Those notations in the log were written by a man with a stiff right thumb."

The federal men exchanged curious glances, for this information verified all they had learned of the supercargo and his past — a strange story that fitted his situation like a glove. He had been a major in the British army in World War I and had been aboard a crowded troopship torpedoed in the Mediterranean. McLellan and two others were the only survivors. By clinging to a floating spar in the surging waters for two terror-filled days and nights he had kept himself alive until he was rescued by the crew of a passing vessel.

Wracked in body and mind, he had spent months in an army hospital suffering from the effects of his ordeal. One of the lasting results was a stiffening of certain joints of his body, one of which was his right thumb. After his discharge from the hospital, McLellan had looked about for work and finally accepted his post aboard the *Quadra*. But he did not know that his troublesome thumb would haunt him.

Its strange role in linking him to the bootlegging conspiracy was described by Heinrich when he took the witness stand in March 1925 as the government's star witness against the crew of the *Quadra*, which, of course, included McLellan.

The expert brought with him a huge bundle of photographs — enlargements of many individual letters in the writing of both Baraciola and the supercargo. Speaking slowly, his eyes fixed on the jury, he explained in the manner of a college professor the distinguishing peculiarities in the writing that had brought him to his conclusions. The jurors appeared to be especially interested in his comments about McLellan's thumb, and the prosecutor pressed for more specific information about the ship's log and its author.

"I can explain it this way," Heinrich replied. "All the writing in this book by this writer shows, when we consider the oval movements, that the writer's thumb does not coordinate properly with the fingers. It is weakest on the retreat movements, in which the fingers are dominant in movement on the downward stroke, and strongest on the movements to the right or the right oblique upward, where the thumb dominates. The result is, because of the thumb's lack of coordination, that in oval movements this writer, instead of a curve, makes his ovals with a hexagon. These are the peculiarities that make me so certain in my identification of the subject's writing."

The jury, obviously impressed, returned a verdict finding all the defendants guilty with the exception of eighteen men, who apparently were considered mere dupes in the operation.

Appeals were taken at once, and the case finally reached the United States Supreme Court on the defense's contention that a new treaty with Great Britain had abrogated the previous one that had fixed the limit of American jurisdiction on the high seas as twelve miles. The new agreement, the attorneys cited, fixed the limit as "one hour's sailing distance" from American territory, and they argued that this had not been violated.

The high court ruled for the government. Heavy sentences were imposed, but all the convicted men excepting McLellan had chosen to cheat the law by disappearing and forfeiting their bail. He paid a moderate fine and started out to look for another job.

No account of forgery and disputed documents would be complete without mention of typewriters, for they often play an important role in this investigative field. Since forgery is properly defined as "something made or written falsely to deceive," one may "forge" a single line, a letter, or a document on a typewriter.

Almost since writing machines were first invented, criminalists have developed means of detecting changes in typing and have succeeded in matching a typewritten word or line with the individual typewriter that produced it. In some cases, though they are rare, the date on a forged document has preceded by years the date of manufacture of the typewriter with which it was written. Typewriting, studied under the microscope, reveals infinitesimal imperfections or irregularities in letter formations — an effective way of linking the writing to the machine. No two machines, even of the same make, model, and age, write exactly alike.

Many experts in this very specialized field have in their laboratories hundreds of specimens of the work of the many typewriters manufactured in the United States and in foreign countries. The FBI excels in this area, as it does in so many other areas of scientific crime detection. Its files contain probably the most extensive collection of typewriting in the world. Each year manufacturers send to the FBI headquarters samples of writing made on the latest models of their equipment.

In this way FBI technicians are able to look at the typing

on a sheet of paper, consult their records, and in an incredibly
short time determine the make of the machine that wrote it,
the name of the model, and the year in which it left the factory.

This phase of police laboratory work has become so precise
that typewriter evidence is now admitted by the courts in most
countries.

Chapter 10

Forgeries on Canvas

FORGERS OF PAINTINGS and sculpture who imitate the works of old masters are in a class by themselves. They are swindlers, but they differ in many respects from the man who signs another's name to a check or a legal document. For one thing, they are knowledgeable in the field of art, its history, and its techniques. For another, they know that their deception must often stand the scrutiny of connoisseurs if they are to profit and escape prison. Therefore, their peculiar type of crime requires unusual cleverness and a high degree of expertise.

The history of art crimes abounds with many fantastic accounts of brazen forgeries that have reaped profits for the offenders and defrauded dedicated, well-intentioned collectors. Yet it was not until a few years ago that a noted California chemist and a resourceful art patron, acting as skilled criminalists, came together to develop the use of fingerprints to detect the forging of paintings.

First, however, we should look into the past to understand the trickery of forgers who prey on art lovers.

Of these, none was more brazen and skillful than Hans van Meegeren, a talented Dutch painter who turned to forgery to avenge himself against critics of his work rather than for financial gain. As a child he had an unusual aptitude for drawing, and his parents decreed that he should become an architect, but rebelling against their wishes, he turned to painting. In the early 1900's he studied under a talented tutor who impressed his young student with the need for meticulous attention to technique and understanding of how the famous artists had used their paints.

With this knowledge and much practice the young student turned out his first art works for public display, only to receive bitter treatment from the critics. As he continued painting

Is it authentic?

with the hope of better results, the critics became increasingly hostile, and the artist, stung by frustration, turned angrily against them, declaring publicly that they did not know good art from bad. His hatred soon became an obsession.

It was unfortunate for van Meegeren that by chance he should meet a starving artist with similar attitudes. This man proudly boasted of having deceived his severest critics and proved their "ignorance." He confessed to having forged the name of Rembrandt on a canvas of his own. It had been acclaimed as one of the greatest works of the famous artist.

As van Meegeren laughed at the story, an idea suddenly took hold; he would gain revenge in an even better and more profitable way. He would produce his own version of an old master's painting, win official recognition, sell it for a good price, and tear up the check. The critics, he was certain, would be mortified. But his scheme would take time, patience, and practice.

On the verge of bankruptcy, he moved to the Riviera where he supported himself for the next four years by painting portraits of tourists. However, he was devoting every spare hour not only to studying the techniques of the great masters but also to trying to learn how he could simulate age on the canvases he produced. Such a project, he knew, would require him to use the same kind of paint they had worked with; certainly he could not risk using modern pigments. So he set about meticulously accomplishing his purpose in ways that he had to discover by himself. For example, he produced his blues by grinding lapis lazuli, and for other colors he resorted to the methods of the old school.

Finally he found a way to harden his paints to give them an ancient look. But he still was not ready to implement his scheme. To avoid any possible imperfections, he purchased a cheap painting done by an obscure artist and studied its frame, its canvas, and even the tacks holding the canvas to the frame. At last he was ready to start.

Imitating the style and techniques of the great, van Meegeren set to work on a canvas that he titled "Disciples at Emmaus," and when the work was finished six months later he boldly forged the name of Vermeer.

The painting, acclaimed by critics and art patrons as one of the greatest finds of the celebrated Vermeer, was sold for 50,000 pounds sterling. Putting aside his earlier intention, the forger pocketed the check and decided to continue his spurious work. In all he produced eight imitations, to each of which he signed the name of a celebrated artist. The last one caught the fancy of Herman Goering, one of Adolf Hitler's right-hand men, who purchased it for the equivalent of half a million dollars. Thus began the forger's undoing.

World War II was over, and allied investigators came upon van Meegeren's forged canvas "Woman Taken in Adultery," bearing Vermeer's signature, hanging in Hitler's Berchtesgarden retreat. At once they asked themselves whose traitorous hands had made this possible. They traced the sale to van Meegeren, who was arrested for dealing with the enemy and selling to the Nazi leader an invaluable painting by a Dutch artist. Trapped at last, the forger sought to save himself from a treason charge by confessing that he had not only painted the canvas in question but eight others.

It remained for a carefully selected group of experts from the Central Laboratory of Belgian Museums to verify the confession. Resorting to microscopes and other scientific equipment, they established that van Meegeren had indeed told the truth. Their minute examinations disclosed imperfections that had escaped the careful eyes of the buyers.

The x-ray revealed that the forger had overpainted his works and that in several he had not taken the trouble to remove the original paint. There were other detectable flaws, like the presence of India ink in places where dust would have gathered in the years since Vermeer's death in 1675. Next the inquisitors turned to the spectograph, which revealed even further proof of forgery.

Van Meegeren's conviction on fraud charges was for him a victory. At last he could laugh at his critics. He was sentenced to a year in prison, a penalty that he gladly accepted, but fate was to intercede. Before his term had started he fell ill and died.

His downfall, however, has not deterred others from following in his footsteps, all of them confident of escaping detection. Art experts say that the number of paintings purchased as genuine Rembrandts is many times more than the number painted by the artist and that the forged works of Van Dyck exceed 2,000. Marc Chagall has also been imitated innumerable times. So greatly has the market been flooded with spurious paintings that the attorney general of California in 1969 began official action against modern-day forgers. As a result of his widespread investigation many paintings have been removed from the walls of popular galleries. More than that, a number of income-tax payers have found themselves thwarted in their efforts to save money by claiming deductions for faked canvases they had given to museums as "charitable gifts."

The exposure of art swindlers, however, has not been confined to California. In Texas a wealthy oilman was found to have one of the largest collections of forged paintings in the possession of one individual, and in recent years experts at New York's Metropolitan Museum admitted that a statue of a horse, thought to be a priceless example of ancient Greek sculpture, had been made only three decades before it was placed on display.

Now, at long last, a scientific means of exposing those who forge the paintings of present-day artists has been developed. It embodies the principle of fingerprinting, and while it will not protect those who purchase spurious works of the old masters, it will at least spare prospective buyers from fraud at the hands of those who choose to imitate contemporary painters.

Credit for this new method belongs to Allmore Aaron, a prominent California collector, and Henry H. Nelson, a chemist of the same state. The idea first came to Aaron a few years ago after his trained eyes had detected a forged canvas imitating the work of a widely known western artist of the present day. Aaron, who had read extensively of the van Meegeren scandal and similar frauds, was approached one morning in his San Francisco gallery by a man offering to sell a fairly large collection of seascapes by Robert Wood, a well-known California artist with whom Aaron was acquainted.

"I'm out of cash," the affable stranger announced. "Name your price; I'll sacrifice them for any reasonable offer."

Aaron, only moderately interested, looked over the collection and shook his head; he already had a number of canvases by Wood. The would-be seller was persistent, however, and he suggested that the dealer look them over a second time. "You'll never get such an offer again," he asserted. Reluctantly the connoisseur agreed, and as his visitor held up one canvas after another, Aaron's gaze fell on one that suddenly aroused his suspicion.

"Let's have a longer look at that one," Aaron requested, and as he eyed it thoughtfully he realized that he had seen the same seascape less than a fortnight before in a Santa Barbara gallery, where it was being shown by the painter himself. His curiosity aroused, Aaron inquired of his visitor where he had been showing the canvases recently.

"I haven't," replied the other. "They've been in my attic for months. They'd still be there if I didn't need the money right now."

Aaron was cautious enough not to reveal his thoughts. He merely told the man that he would think it over. A few days later, however, he related the matter to his brother Len, insisting that there should be some way of protecting buyers from such brazen forgery. The more he thought about it, the more determined he became to achieve his purpose.

The problem engaged his attention for many weeks before he finally determined on a course of action. "If fingerprints can nab burglars and even murderers," he reasoned, "why can't they be used to protect us from art forgers?"

For technical advice he decided to consult Nelson, the chemist, and in the latter's southern California office Aaron explained his problem. "Isn't there some scientific way," he inquired, "for a painter to identify his canvas by a fingerprint — some way to do it so that the print can't be altered, erased, or forged?"

Nelson requested time to think it over. Weeks passed before he sent for Aaron. When the two were together again, the chemist announced that after much laboratory work he had evolved a foolproof way of protecting paintings from forgers.

"Tell me how?" Aaron asked excitedly. "It seems too good to be true."

Nelson opened a desk drawer and took out a little bottle. "This is obviously a chemical — my own preparation," he began. "In far more tests than were necessary I've applied this solution to the back of a painting. It works its way into the fabric regardless of whether it is canvas or linen but, mind you, it can't go all the way through. The painting itself cannot be harmed."

"And then what?" Aaron pressed.

"The rest is simple. After this liquid has been applied to a small section of the back of the canvas, the artist inks his thumb and makes a clear print over the area. This mark is then covered with a sealer. Once that's applied the thumbprint can never be removed or altered without completely ruining the picture."

Aaron was elated but he still wondered how to relate such a process to his major problem. The answer was not long in coming.

Aaron proposed that the artist's thumbprint be placed on cards which then would be sent to various places of business and placed in security safes. An additional copy of the thumbprint would be kept in a bank vault.

Aaron was anxious to emphasize that this method, effective as it has proved, still cannot protect buyers of forged canvases of the old masters — but it does definitely safeguard those who purchase the latest works of modern artists.

He is hopeful, however, that in time some resourceful person may discover a technique to determine the genuineness of paintings claimed to be the work of early-day artists. To illustrate this need he cited the case of a prominent Texas multi-millionaire, a generous patron of the arts, who spent more than $1,500,000 in purchasing paintings purported to be the works of such masters as Picasso, Derain and others. Many of these he generously presented to the art museum named in his honor at Southern Methodist University.

For these gifts he received unbounded thanks until art critics viewed the "rare paintings," shrugged their shoulders and agreed unanimously that they were rank forgeries.

Aside from paintings, Aaron is still also eager to learn a way to detect forgeries in sculpture represented as the work of famed artists. In this regard he is quick to mention the disappointment suffered by officials of New York's famed Metropolitan Museum who were elated when they received the gift of a sculptured horse said to be hundreds of years old.

Its presence at the museum attracted wide attention among art patrons until it was learned, some time later, that the work had been done only thirty years before.

The authenticity of paintings, however, is Aaron's main concern, probably because he knows that the number of canvases actually purchased as the genuine works of Rembrandt is actually ten times greater than the total number of paintings ever produced by the artist and that the number of spurious Van Dycks is even greater. Even Chagall, he declares, has been widely imitated.

Chapter 11

Medics on the Stand

E VERY DAY IN THE COURTS of law physicians, surgeons or specialists in one of the many fields of medicine are called to the witness stand. The case may be a damage suit over an accident or a murder trial. Regardless of the issue, the doctor's testimony assumes major importance and is often the turning point in a complicated controversy.

Depending on the nature of the case, the doctor may be called on to discuss bone structure, corpuscles in human blood, the nature of a wound, or the composition of a hair. Perhaps rigor mortis will require an expert's opinion. In any circumstance, the doctor must explain in highly technical terms in a way that any layman on the jury can comprehend.

The doctor's role symbolizes the close relationship that has existed between medicine and the law for many centuries. The practice of forensic medicine derives its name from the fact that this is the medicine of the forum or the law court. Actually forensic medicine is defined by one attorney as "the application of medical knowledge to the administration of law and the furthering of justice"; it is as old as civilization itself. Through the ages the law has influenced medicine, and medicine has affected the law in the codes of different societies. Certain cases already referred to in this book, such as the murder of the French bailiff, Gouffe, in which hairs were an important element, are perfect illustrations of forensic medicine in practice.

Religion, superstition, and magic played a strange part in early times in the relationship of law and medicine. It is said that the functions of the physician and the judge were first united in the priest, who functioned as a liaison between God and man. This was at a time when sickness and death were considered perhaps to be divine punishment for the failure to observe divine law, or even the result of evil spirits.

The code of Hammurabi of Babylon in about 2200 B.C., regarded as the oldest set of established principles, defined the
rights and duties of medical practitioners. Thus did legal or
forensic medicine first come into being. From about the start of
the Christian era, India went some steps further. By government decree, the drunk, insane, fatigued, and those with impaired sense organs, were barred as legal witnesses. China as
early as 3000 B.C. published information on poisons, including
arsenic and opium.

Of the ancient civilizations, Greece appears to have been an
exception in the acceptance of legal medicine. Because dead
bodies were regarded as sacred autopsies were forbidden, but in
a five-year period ending in 355 B.C. the famous Hippocrates
spoke extensively on the legal responsibility for wounds and
their relation to death. One of the most famous assassinations
in early times, the murder of Julius Caesar, called for a postmortem examination as a legal procedure though the con-
spirators faced trial only on the battlefield. The physician who
examined the bleeding body concluded that only one of the
twenty-three wounds was mortal.

Ironically, the Germanic and Slavic peoples who overthrew
the Roman Empire in western Europe in the fifth century —
tribes that were generally regarded as barbaric — were the first
to declare by statute that medical experts were needed in legal
disputes. An individual found guilty of injuring another was
obliged to pay an indemnity, and the nature of the wound became an important factor requiring medical judgment.

Then, as the centuries passed, the role of medicine in legal
affairs assumed greater importance. In 1575 Ambroise Pare,
known as the father of French surgery, wrote a book that attracted wide attention having to do with medico-legal cases
involving death or serious injury.

Strangely, some years later, a new book appeared that represented a retrograde step. In Germany Andreas Libuvius re-
verted to post-Roman-Empire days, elaborating on the value of
an ancient test of a murder suspect's guilt. Suspects would be
made to touch the bodies of the victims; if they were guilty
blood would flow from the dead person's wounds. This method
won the approval of King James VI of Scotland, but fortunately
it did not hinder the progress of forensic medicine.

In the middle of the seventeenth century in Rome, Paulus Zacchias, celebrated for his work in the medico-legal field and physician to Pope Innocent X, wrote a series of books that marked a most significant advance. Less than a century afterward, Samuel Parr of England won wide acclaim with a book regarded as the first systematic work on medical jurisprudence.

Of the many outstanding modern-day authorities in the field, none has gained greater recognition in America than Dr. Le Moyne Snyder of Paradise, California, who is constantly called from one state to another for his expert opinion, as in the celebrated case of Dr. Sam Shepard. Dr. Snyder occupies a position of eminence in this country equal to that accorded in England to the late Sir Bernard Pilsbury, who is regarded as one of the greatest pathologists of all time, a man of science whose skills solved many baffling crimes.

Being a physician and a lawyer, Dr. Snyder is a member of both the American Medical and the American Bar associations. In this book, *Homicide Investigation*, he cites the necessity for forensic medicine, stating that "approximately 20 percent of all persons die under circumstances that require an official inquiry into the cause of death." Therefore the medicolegal practitioner must learn the secrets that teeth, bones, muscle, blood, and other physical factors can yield.

Because of his professional skills in two fields, Dr. Snyder some years ago became a member of an informal and dedicated group of volunteers and unpaid investigators calling themselves the Court of Last Resort. This organization was founded by Dr. Snyder's friend, the late Erle Stanley Gardner, the author of the Perry Mason mysteries, and Henry Steeger, a magazine publisher. Serving with them, also as volunteers, were Raymond Schindler, a widely known private detective, B. J. (Bob) Rhay, and Tom Smith (the latter two were skilled in penology and sociology).

No example of Dr. Snyder's skill is more fascinating than his role in a particularly unusual murder case in which the exact time of a woman's death became the all-important element in determining the guilt or innocence of a man in prison. In making that decision Dr. Snyder demonstrated the practice of forensic medicine at its highest and most technical level.

The crime occurred in Pottstown, Pennsylvania, where the

body of Mrs. Miriam Greene, a twenty-seven-year-old employee of a tire plant, was found at two o'clock on a Monday
afternoon, December 9, 1946. Her landlady had entered the unfortunate woman's apartment with a pass key after word came
that Mrs. Greene, usually scrupulous about her working time,
had not appeared at her desk. A blue scarf tied tightly about her
neck indicated that she had been strangled.

The police responded promptly, and while they awaited the
coroner they made two hasty observations — the woman had
been dead for a considerable time, and robbery could not have
been the killer's motive since a large amount of jewelry had
been left untouched. Inquiries to neighbors in the building
were of no help. No one could recall having heard unusual
noises in the apartment; in fact they knew little of Mrs. Greene
except that she was a quiet person who minded her own affairs.

In trying to establish the approximate time of the murder,
the police ran into their first conflict. The autopsy surgeon was
of the opinion that Mrs. Greene had died on Sunday, the day
before her body was recovered, but a doctor who had been
summoned by the landlady and had been the first to see the
body thought death might have occurred on Monday. This difference of opinion definitely hindered the work of the police,
who at this time were concerned with statements from two
men — Mrs. Greene's former husband, George, and a friend,
George Wentzel, who held a position of trust in a die casting
works in Pottstown.

Greene was of little assistance, stating that he had not seen
his former wife for a long time, but he did mention the name of
Wentzel, with whom Mrs. Greene, he had been told, was keeping company. When Wentzel was questioned he first insisted
that he had been only slightly acquainted with the woman, but
in a second interview he acknowledged that he had not told the
truth. He now admitted that there had been something of a
love affair. He had lied before, he explained, to keep the affair
from his wife.

When the investigators pressed him further, Wentzel finally
told them that he had called at Mrs. Greene's apartment on the
Sunday night before her body was found and that she was dead.
He fixed the time at about eleven o'clock.

"Why didn't you notify the police?" he was asked.

Wentzel thought for a moment before answering. "As a married man I didn't want to get involved in a murder case. I was sure someone else would find her before too long."

The questioning continued, and when Wentzel realized that he was being regarded as a suspect he bluntly announced that he had an airtight alibi. "If you really think I did it," he exclaimed, "go and talk to my pals in the gun club. I was on a hunting trip with them from Thursday afternoon until I left them to go to Miriam's place late Sunday night like I told you. And we were hundreds of miles out of town."

He gave the officers the names and addresses of his fifteen companions who, he said, would substantiate his statement. Each member of the hunting party was interviewed separately, and each corroborated what Wentzel had said about his absence from the city, including the hours involved. Nevertheless, with Wentzel as the only suspect, the police decided after further checking to charge him with murder and let a jury decide on the circumstantial evidence. Wentzel, still pleading his innocence, was confident of a quick acquittal.

The pivotal point in the trial, as had been expected, was the exact time of Mrs. Greene's death, the state contending that Wentzel had killed her at the time he claimed to have discovered the body. To support his theory the autopsy surgeon testified that in his judgment death could have occurred between twelve and twenty-four hours before he had first seen the body at seven o'clock on Monday evening. But under defense cross-examination, he admitted that the victim might have been dead for seventy-two hours. Further doubt was cast on the time of death by a prominent mortician, called by the defense, who swore that Mrs. Greene had probably been dead for fully eighty hours when she was found.

The court's instructions favored the defense, but to Wentzel's astonishment the jury found him guilty of murder in the second degree. He was sentenced to serve from ten to twenty years in Pennsylvania Pennitentiary. Appeals to higher courts failed and Wentzel faced a dismal future, convinced that he was doomed to spend years in prison for a crime he insisted he had not committed.

This doubtlessly would have been his fate but for the help of Dr. Snyder and forensic medicine. His entry into the case was strange and unexpected. To Wentzel's surprise the mother and sister of the victim suddenly came forward in his defense, pub-

licly declaring their belief in his innocence. The mother, Mrs.
Katy O'Mara, and the sister, Mrs. Eckenroth, went still
further; they offered a large reward for the apprehension of the
murderer, and they appealed to the Court of Last Resort for
help.

Gardner, working with Rhay and Smith, inquired into the
case and gradually became convinced that it warranted much
more time and effort. They also realized that the final judgment must come through forensic medicine.

They interviewed many co-workers of Mrs. Greene at the
tire plant and located two women who had walked with her to
her apartment on Friday evening. So far as could be learned, no
one had seen her alive after that. Company records showed
that she had not reported for work on Saturday and had not
called the plant to say that she would be absent, though on previous occasions she had always telephoned to explain her
absence.

Pressing the inquiry further, the investigators were told by
Mrs. Greene's mother that her daughter was in the habit of visiting her every Saturday night after work and never failed to
telephone if this was not possible.

With this information, Gardner and his associates were convinced that the murder had taken place on Friday and not on
the following Saturday as the police claimed. Their conclusion
was strengthened by a report showing that when the body was
found clothing that Mrs. Greene had worn to work on Friday
lay neatly folded on her bed.

The time had now come for Dr. Snyder to turn to science, to
determine through his technical knowledge just when death
had occurred. He had made such investigations many times before. His first move, however, was in another direction. Taking
a lie detector to the prison, he proceeded, with Wentzel's full
approval, to use it in determining the veracity of the prisoner's
statement. When the test was over, the polygraph's recordings
showed that the convicted man had told the truth in response
to every question.

For the next week or more Dr. Snyder delved into the strictly
medical aspects of the problem. At his direction Rhay and
Smith had gathered a vast fund of information, including the
temperature of the apartment when the body was found, the
outside temperature, the atmospheric conditions, and the

state of the remains, as well as all the medical testimony given at the trial. With all this at hand, Dr. Snyder sought to determine the precise time of death.

His conclusions were presented in a long and technical report that began with a dissertation on body changes after the last breath. In this context he reviewed the testimony of the autopsy surgeon and the other medical men at the trial, taking serious issue with all their findings, which he insisted were entirely at variance with the time they had fixed for Mrs. Greene's demise. To substantiate his opinions, he carefully cited established medical knowledge concerning the changes in a corpse after death.

Referring specifically to the time issue, he wrote that "to intelligently appraise this problem, one must have some understanding of the mechanism of death due to strangulation." He delved into the subject of rigor mortis, explaining that it involves "a stiffening of all muscle tissue due to chemical changes which take place [after death] in the body itself." These changes, he asserted, do not take effect over the entire body until eight to twelve hours after death, and they remain for from twelve to twenty-four hours, after which they begin to disappear. After another eight to ten hours they are gone, he pointed out.

Using this as his basic premise he turned to the case before him with a question and an answer:

If Mrs. Greene had met her death at eleven o'clock Sunday night, December 8 [the state's contention] by strangulation, what would have been the expected findings when the body was discovered at 2 P.M. the following day and autopsied five hours later?

Fifteen minutes after death the entire body would have been extremely rigid due to rigor mortis, while the face, neck and probably the shoulders might be somewhat dusky in color.

This, he reasoned, failed to coincide with the testimony at the trial, and in support of his contention he cited the autopsy surgeon's report on the body temperature five hours after it was found. He then declared that the usual "loss of one degree per hour after death in relation to room temperature" belied the testimony of that witness. It was a conclusion that he was able to reach only by taking into consideration what he had

learned of the physical condition of the apartment, the effect of
a partly opened window, the amount of steam heat, and other
conditions of equal importance.

He reached this final conclusion:

Considering all the facts involved, and based on the
time the body was autopsied — 7 P.M. December 9, 1946
— it is highly improbable that death had occurred less
than forty-eight hours previously, and it is my belief
that Mrs. Greene expired from sixty to eighty hours before she was observed by the autopsy surgeon.

His report, written with as little technical terminology as
possible, was sent to the Board of Pardons and Paroles of
Pennsylvania and was carefully studied. The result was as Dr.
Snyder and his colleagues had expected. The board, by unanimous vote, called on Governor John S. Fine to grant Wentzel an
unconditional pardon and this was done. Forensic medicine,
interpreted by an expert, had opened prison doors for an innocent man, and though the murderer was never apprehended
justice triumphed.

Equally outstanding was the achievement of England's Sir
Bernard Pilsbury in sending the guilty Dr. Crippen to the gallows. Though many decades have passed since that tragedy
filled columns in English newspapers, it is still remembered
for its two highly significant elements. Not only did it demonstrate again the importance of forensic medicine, but it also
marked the first time that a new invention — wireless telegraphy — was used to apprehend a fugitive.

Dr. Crippen, an American physician born in Coldwater,
Michigan in 1862, had married a Polish beauty named Kuni-
gunde Mackamotski, a dominating woman with high ambitions to become an operatic star but with little if any talent.
Nevertheless she had beguiled her adoring husband into believing that she had a brilliant future on the stage. He paid for
the best teachers, and as a further token of his love he bought
her diamonds and expensive clothes.

When in 1900 Mrs. Crippen had made no progress in achiev-
ing her ambitions, she persuaded her husband to move with
her to London for there, she insisted, her talents would be ap-
preciated — a hope that failed to materialize.

In England Dr. Crippen soon established himself as the head
of an agency for a patent medicine manufacturer, and his wife,

taking the stage name of Cora Turner, succeeded in getting an engagement to sing in a music hall. On her first appearance she was hissed off the stage, and when it became impossible to obtain other bookings she turned bitterly against her husband, blaming him for her failure. Still hopeful of success, she insisted on intruding herself into musical circles and gradually turned her affections to other men.

After ten years of abuse and humiliation, the doctor, then fifty years of age, became interested in his secretary, vivacious twenty-year-old Ethel Le Neve, and a romance followed in spite of the wife's protests. She often threatened to leave him, saying that if she did she would take all the money in their joint bank account.

As far as friends knew the Crippens were going their separate ways, and their troubles did not receive public attention until one morning in June 1910, when Chief Inspector Walter Dew received a call from a young man who reported that Mrs. Crippen had dropped from sight early in February and that her absence called for investigation. He said that she had last been seen on January 31 leaving a party. To add to the mystery, the caller related that a few days after this a musical society had received a letter from her stating that she was leaving for California. The message, however, was not in her handwriting.

Inspector Dew lost no time in launching an official inquiry. First he interviewed friends of the couple, who stated that while Dr. Crippen had been reluctant to discuss his affairs, they had seen him at a dance with Ethel, who was wearing Mrs. Crippen's best gown and some of her jewels. They had still more to say: the doctor had first told them that his wife had fled to California with a wealthy man but later they had received mourning cards announcing her demise. Ethel had already moved into Crippen's residence.

The detective then interviewed Crippen, who said that his wife was still alive; he had concocted the story of her death because of his humiliation over her departure with a rival. At his suggestion, Dew accompanied him to his home and searched it, but there appeared to be no clue to the whereabouts of the missing wife.

Dew was now ready to dismiss the matter as another domestic situation, but before doing so he decided to pay one more visit to the Crippen residence. It was vacant and so was the doctor's office. The inspector was beginning to feel that he had erred in his judgment, and he returned to the home on Hilldrop Crescent determined to subject it to an intensive search. He had nearly completed his work without any results when he came to the basement. There to his surprise he discovered a few loose bricks in the flooring.

Hastily removing them, he found soft dirt and began to dig. He had not gone far before he uncovered what was obviously part of a human body. The head and limbs were missing, but adhering to the decaying flesh was a woman's garment.

Dew realized the significance of his discovery and sent at once for Dr. Augustuc Pepper, a well-known pathologist working closely with Scotland Yard. Dr. Pepper removed what remained of the corpse and at almost first glance perceived that it had been mutilated by someone familiar with anatomy. Almost all the bones had been removed, as had all parts of the body that would indicate sex, although a few remaining hairs appeared to be those of a woman.

The police felt that this must be a part of the body of the missing Mrs. Crippen, but how to prove it vexed Scotland Yard. Friends viewed the garment but could only say that it looked something like the kind worn by Mrs. Crippen. Now, with no other evidence at hand, Dew and Pepper reckoned that forensic medicine must be put to the test and that it remained for skilled medical men rather than detectives to establish the victim's identity in a way that would convince a jury.

Meanwhile the missing Dr. Crippen and Ethel had to be found. Detailed descriptions of the pair were broadcast throughout England with orders for their immediate arrest, and now the Yard had a new facility — wireless telegraphy, which had never before been used in a manhunt. In the belief that the couple may have fled to America, radio was used to alert all ships putting out of English ports. Dr. Crippen was pictured as fifty years of age, five feet three inches tall, with scant sandy hair and a scraggly moustache. It was further noted that he wore gold-rimmed eyeglasses and that he revealed false teeth when smiling.

Among the many vessels reached by wireless was the British steamer *Montrose*, whose captain read the instructions and ordered all his officers to keep a sharp lookout for the wanted couple. When the ship stopped at Antwerp, he personally scrutinized the passengers who came aboard for the Atlantic voyage, and soon his suspicions centered on two people — a man registered as John Robinson, accompanied by a younger person listed as his son John.

The captain watched them closely and soon became convinced that they were not acting like father and son: John's table manners were definitely effeminate. A message was sent by wireless to Scotland Yard, and Inspector Dew was dispatched to board the *Laurentia* at Liverpool; it was to reach Quebec in advance of the *Montrose*.

The Robinsons were arrested at once. As had been suspected, young John proved to be no other than Ethel Le Neve, and her older companion was easily recognized as Dr. Crippen. They were returned to London for trial, neither knowing then what the laboratory had disclosed in their absence.

Dr. Pepper, carefully examining the mass of bloody flesh and tissue taken from the cellar, had found a small strip of skin barely more than five inches square. Studying it under the microscope, he discovered what he believed might be a scar from abdominal surgery but he was far from certain. His suspicions increased on learning that Mrs. Crippen had once undergone a hysterectomy operation.

For assistance he summoned Dr. Pilsbury, who by then had gained a national reputation in his field. Pilsbury at the outset realized that he was undertaking one of the most difficult tasks in his career, for the strip of skin provided little with which to work. It would be useless unless he could establish that it had come from the abdominal area, and that would necessitate finding some tiny identifiable bit of muscle or tissue.

For days he compared the skin fragment with specimens of abdominal walls, checking one against the other until finally he was convinced that the piece he was working with had actually come from the abdomen. Now it remained for him to determine the nature of the scar and whether it had resulted from surgery.

When he had completed his technical tests, he was thoroughly satisfied that this had been the case. And the microscope had provided even more evidence than expected — it revealed close to the scar tissue a tiny and almost imperceptible imprint of the texture of the garment, which had been pressed against the surrounding skin. Laboratory studies yielded still more evidence. An examination of the vital organs disclosed that Mrs. Crippen had evidently died from overdoses of a poisonous drug occasionally used in anesthesia. Its purchase was traced to Crippen.

There remained little hope for the defense when the accused doctor came to trial in October 1910. His attorney had no other recourse than to attack the Crown's case on two points. First, he contended that the body was not that of Mrs. Crippen and that the grim remains had been buried in the cellar long before the accused physician had rented the house. And to further confuse the jury, he challenged the findings of Dr. Pilsbury, insisting that the bit of skin used by the prosecution as one of its most important pieces of evidence had actually come from a thigh. Two physicians testified in support of this claim, but when Dr. Pilsbury took the stand to refute them it was apparent that the jurors fully accepted his version.

Dr. Crippen was found guilty of murder, and the judge, placing the customary black cap to his head, pronounced the death sentence. Less then a month later the doctor mounted the scaffold. As for young Ethel Le Neve, she was freed when the authorities satisfied themselves that she had no knowledge of what Dr. Crippen had done. She opened a dressmaking shop in London and tried to forget her involvement in a case that had attracted such wide attention on two continents.

Chapter 12

The Hunt for the Truth

THERE IS AN ANCIENT SAYING by the Jewish sages: "Truth is the seal of God." In another sense, truth is the major goal of criminal justice and law enforcement. Investigators hunt for true and accurate facts; they must check the accused and all witnesses against false or inaccurate statements.

Dr. Hans Gross, whom we already have met as "the father of criminalistics," put the problem succinctly in a paper written in the middle of the nineteenth century. "In a certain sense," he wrote, "a large part of the criminalist's work is nothing more than a battle against lies. He has to discover the truth and must fight the opposite. He meets the opposite at every step."

Through the years the detection of lies has been one of the chief and most vexing problems in law enforcement. Can liars be betrayed only by clever investigative work or can their mental and physical processes be made to trap them? Can science, testing human emotions with mechanical equipment, wring the truth from a person bent on deception?

Experts have sought the answer through a wide range of experiments, until today the lie detector or polygraph, as it is properly called, is in general use in many countries. Though its findings are not yet admissible in courts of law, they do render invaluable aid to police and frequently they bring about confessions.

Some sociologists and theologians question the fairness of the lie detector, arguing that it unjustly robs suspects of their innermost secrets, and some courts have held that to some extent it illegally compels defendants to testify against themselves. Yet modern police authorities insist that many baffling cases have been solved only because such a test, taken voluntarily by a suspect, has proved scientifically that he or she lied in answering key questions pertinent to the case.

A lie detector in use at the Federal Bureau of Investigation

Dr. John A. Larson, who contributed a great deal to the development and practical use of the apparatus, cites some ancient methods used to reveal lying — methods like those followed by King Solomon to determine which of two women was telling the truth in claiming a child as her own. By ordering the child to be cut in two, the wise ruler decided that the trustful woman was the one who willingly relinquished her claim to save a life; the liar kept her tongue. Larson also points to a later Oriental custom in which a mouthful of rice was fed to a suspected person, who was deemed guilty if he or she could not readily spit it out — a test predicated on the fact that fear usually inhibits the secretion of saliva.

In the first part of the nineteenth century, Cesare Lombroso pioneered in experiments with the heartbeat as a means of detecting lying, an interesting forerunner of today's polygraph, which has now advanced far beyond the early concepts of the distinguished Italian, utilizing not only heartbeats but changes in respiration and blood pressure to determine the truth or falsity of an answer.

Proud of his success and certain of the soundness of his theories, Lombroso recorded numbers of effective tests, including one concerning a notorious thief whose heartbeat reactions proved him guilty of one crime and innocent of another. It was on the early Lombrose principle that later criminalists like Vollmer, Keeler, and Larson based their developments of the lie detecting machine, but progress was slow and many methods and theories were tried and abandoned.

Professor Hugo Munsterberg, Harvard's pioneer in criminal psychology, studied long and hard to determine the value of the oath taken by a witness. Having come to hold a dim view of the worth of the conventional oath, Munsterberg wrote in 1907 that while the religious nature of the oath may eliminate an intention to hide the truth, it fails to increase the capacity for truthful statements. He admitted that the oath may help to obtain objective truth, explaining that "it not only suppresses the intentional lie but it focuses the intention on the details of the statement. The witness feels the duty of putting his best will into the effort to reproduce the whole truth and nothing but the truth."

While some were following Lombroso's heartbeat tests, other criminalists like Dr. R. E. House turned in other directions. House held the attention of professional meetings with his discourses on the use of a truth serum — scopolamine — with which he was experimenting; he was convinced that a subject under the influence of the drug would lose all inhibitions and speak only the truth. Unfortunately House, limited in his work by lack of funds, died in the midst of his research still confident that he was working in the right direction. "The day is not far distant," he wrote shortly before his death, "when science will not only prevent 75 percent of crime but convict those who are guilty."

The so-called "association test" commanded attention for a time. Under this procedure, a person suspected of a crime was made to listen to the reading of some one hundred words well prepared in advance. Many of them were wholly unrelated to the crime, but interspersed among them were some that bore directly on the offense involved. Subjects were made to respond to each word with the first idea entering their minds at the moment that the word was spoken. Theoretically, they would incriminate themselves by their answers — or hesitation — when hearing a word associated directly or indirectly with the crime.

Though experiments along this line continued for a time, Munsterberg at Harvard insisted on pressing forward with his attempts to develop the principle of the lie detector. He had many other interests, too, for as a psychologist he was deeply interested in the different versions given by people witnessing the same incident. Seriously questioning the reliability of honest witnesses, he once unexpectedly jumped from his desk in the midst of a classroom recital and fired a revolter three times into the air. No two students gave the same account of what had occurred. If intelligent, supposedly observant people differed so widely in what they had seen, he reasoned, what could be expected of people of a low mentality, especially if they wanted to deceive. He became more concerned than ever with the need for a scientific method for detecting falsehoods.

The most far-reaching and effective work in developing the lie detector reached its climax in about 1920 through the efforts of Chief of Police August Vollmer of Berkeley, California, and one of his scientifically minded young policemen, John A. Larson, who later became assistant state criminologist of Illinois and psychiatrist for the Institute of Juvenile Research with degrees in medicine and psychiatry. They were soon joined by a former Los Angeles police officer, Leonardo Keeler, who some years later became a staff member of the Scientific Crime Detection Laboratory connected with Northwestern University.

Vollmer was thoroughly convinced of the practical value of the lie detector, pointing out that it provided the only safe and fair means of determining when a person was lying, especially an old offender long experienced in deceiving his questioners. He often argued that not infrequently a murderer is the first to report the crime, believing that this may divert suspicion.

Working together, the three developed a lie detector that recorded on paper with up-and-down lines a subject's changes in heartbeat, blood pressure, and respiration under steady questioning. The equipment was strapped to the suspect's body in such a way that these changes could be recorded by the rise and fall of a needle on a revolving strip of paper — the theory being that if the subject was lying emotional stresses would cause the lines on the graph to rise above the established normal levels.

Some of the first of their many experiments brought criticism from those who did not comprehend the method, arguing that the tensions and nervousness resulting from the mere awareness of being tested would naturally result in false, misleading indications on the graph. But Vollmer and his colleagues were eager to dispel such misconceptions. They explained, as present operators of the polygraph do, that the testing of a subject begins with a long series of innocuous questions in no way involving the crime. Not until after these have established a normal level of reactions does the examiner subtly and with no voice change ask a "dynamite question," pertaining directly to the offense. The graphic result discloses whether or not the subject is lying.

Even today some operators of the lie detector lack the experience necessary to produce accurate findings, and some errors in conclusions have occurred. The expert criminalist of course endeavors to reduce these to a minimum.

Larson, who in later years recorded many of his early experiments in his book, *Lying and Its Detection*, relates the case of a housewife who reported the theft of a $20 bill from her home, which apparently had been entered through a forced window.

The police were without a clue and questioned a number of people, among them a family friend who was regarded as above suspicion even though he was the last person known to have left the place. After a time he volunteered to take a lie detector test, assuring the officers that he would soon be vindicated.

The graph showed no changes as he answered numbers of unrelated questions — his smoking habits, his job, his taste in movies, and his opinion of dancing. Suddenly he was asked point-blank, "Did you steal a $20 bill?"

"No," he answered, but the needle jumped far above the normal lines, establishing the falsity of his denial. Still neither the investigators nor the family could believe him guilty. A day later, shortly before he was to be eliminated as a suspect, Larson proposed a second test. The results were the same and the family friend, advised of what had occurred, admitted his guilt with the remark, "the machine has the goods on me."

Another of the many cases related by Larson reveals how confessions obtained by the lie detector often lead to the capture of others involved in the same crime or in unsolved earlier offenses. This incident concerns a gang of eight youths from eighteen to twenty years of age who turned holdup men, robbing couples in a "lovers' lane." Only two of the young gangsters were captured, and they stubbornly insisted that they had done nothing wrong. However, when the lie detector tests demonstrated that they were lying, they broke down, admitted their guilt, and named all their accomplices, who were then rounded up and who in their long confessions admitted a number of other crimes of which they had not been suspected.

Shortly after this affair a storekeeper complained to the police that he could no longer endure the steady round of shoplifting that was taking place in his store. Asked for a list of the customers who might be responsible, he named thirty-eight college girls, but he hesitated as he came to one name, explaining that this young woman was the daughter of a wealthy family and would have no reason to steal.

Vollmer and Larson, who had been consulted, decided to test all the girls, including the wealthy one, and the group consented. The testing of the first few brought only negative results, but when the last subject, the girl from the affluent family, was questioned, sudden changes in the machine's graph disclosed unmistakable evidence of false answers. Faced with the results, she confessed, explaining that she could not control a compulsion to steal and had pilfered hundreds of dollars worth of merchandise "just for the thrill," selling her loot for ridiculously little money.

Larson and his associates always took pride in their ability to clear the innocent as well as incriminate the guilty. For example, they often recounted the case of two men jailed as bank robbers. The trial had progressed for several days when the counsel for the defense obtained court permission for a lie detector test.

Despite the polygraph's positive showing that the defendants were telling the truth in denying their guilt, the trial continued. The time for the closing arguments was drawing near when word came from the sheriff that two men, arrested only an hour before, had confessed to the bank robbery, describing the crime in such detail that no doubt could remain of their guilt. The trial ended abruptly, and two innocent prisoners walked out of the courtroom free.

A far better known case of an innocent man vindicated by the lie detector involved a watchman named Gonzalez who was suspected of murder after the burned body of a man was found in the fire-swept laboratory of Charles Henry Schwartz in Walnut Creek, California. Schwartz had established what he claimed was a factory to manufacture artificial silk by his own secret process. In setting fire to the place, in which lay the body of the man he had murdered, Schwartz had deliberately planned to direct suspicion against his watchman, conniving in such a way that Gonzalez would appear to be both an arsonist and a murderer.

However, when hours of questioning failed to shake Gonzalez, he consented to a lie detector test under the direction of both Larson and Vollmer. The results were conclusively in his favor, and his exoneration led to the final solution that betrayed Schwartz as the killer.

Schwartz's ultimate betrayal followed investigations of a vast amount of circumstantial evidence which disclosed, among numerous incriminating facts, that he was heavily in debt and faced a lawsuit resulting from an alleged love affair. He finally shot and killed himself behind locked doors in his apartment as police were threatening to break in. Beside the body lay a note pleading for his wife's forgiveness.

Early work with the lie detector was gaining attention when I, then city editor of a San Francisco daily newspaper, conceived the idea of giving the test to William Hightower, who had been arrested shortly before for the murder of Father Patrick Heslin. Never before had a formally accused murderer in the Far West been subjected to such an examination.

Since Hightower not only insisted that he was innocent but complained bitterly that his assistance to the police in locating the body was unappreciated, he appeared to be a fit subject for the polygraph. He and his lawyer were both consulted by me and they consented without reservation. Because competing morning newspapers "covered" the jail house until midnight, the test was scheduled for two o'clock in the morning.

Under the cover of darkness, Larson and Keeler drove with their paraphernalia to the court house and were admitted to Hightower's cell. He smiled as the straps were adjusted to his body and told the experts that he was grateful for the opportunity to prove his innocence. A number of the usual innocuous questions established a norm on the chart. After some twenty minutes of such interrogation, Hightower was asked abruptly, "Why did you kill Father Heslin?"

"I didn't do it," he replied without the slightest outward show of emotion, but the graph needle, which he could not control, took a sudden jump — in fact it bounded far over the chart, proof to the examiners that he had lied in denying his guilt. Hightower was subsequently convicted of murder and sentenced to life imprisonment.

Much has been written of an extraordinary case in the Pacific Northwest in which one Alfred Lingle was shot to death in a "gang murder." Following long investigation, a man named Bell confessed to his participation in the crime and implicated another man named Sullivan as an accomplice. His story raised grave doubts, and a lie detector test, directed by Larson, indicated that Bell's entire account was false. Subsequent investigation led to the conclusion that Bell had lied deliberately, implicating Sullivan because he had stolen Bell's sweetheart and deserted him after his arrest.

Can a clever suspect fool the lie detector? The question has often been asked. The answer seems to be that such a person can deceive an inexperienced operator of the machine but not an expert. An example was provided some years ago in a widely publicized mystery when a shrewd murderer twice misled the lie detector only to have his guilt proved in a third test given by an experienced operator.

Involved in the final solution of the case were other elements in crime laboratory procedure, like the evidence yielded by a few little pieces of string and a single blood spot on a leather jacket. But in spite of these corroborating factors, the case deserves attention here because of the unusual and ironic part played by the polygraph.

The murder came to light on a warm March afternoon in 1960 when a party of boys, tramping through Starved Rock Park, a popular recreation area in La Salle County, Illinois, discovered the brutally beaten bodies of three well-dressed women lying in a small cave in an unfrequented part of the grounds. Horrified, they ran to the nearest telephone and notified the state police.

The atrociousness of the crime became immediately apparent to the first officers reaching the scene. The bodies, covered with blood, had obviously been dragged some distance. Two of them were bound together at the wrist and ankle with tightly tied white cord. Their clothing had been pulled over their waists and their underwear torn to shreds, giving the appearance of a sex crime. This conclusion was strengthened by the fact that the victims' jewelry had not been taken and their handbags were intact. A length of tree bough, stained with blood, lay close by, evidently the killer's weapon.

It did not take long to identify the victims by credit cards in their bags, disclosing them to be the middle-aged wives of prominent Chicago businessmen. Inquiry at the nearby Starved Rock Lodge, an exclusive resort, revealed that the women had arrived in a station wagon and had last been seen walking toward the park's recreation area.

A careful examination of the ground produced no clues. A number of bloodstains were valueless to the police since they had been smeared with dirt, and a later scrutiny of the lethal weapon showed no fingerprints. The only apparent leads were the string and the peculiar knots, but the state police, assuming full charge of the investigation, belittled these as of no value. They were leaning strongly toward a theory that Chicago gangsters were responsible, for at this time gang violence had reached a serious level.

Following this reasoning, the police called on the Chicago authorities for help, urging a careful checking of gang members recently discharged from prison. This procedure created a schism with Harlan D. Warren, the State attorney for La Salle County, who had taken a deep interest in the case although he had neither jurisdiction nor responsibility for the investigation. His duty lay solely in prosecuting whoever would be charged with the murders, but he was not one to sit idly by with no concern for the importance of prosecution evidence.

Warren had persistently urged that a scientific study of the string and knots might provide an important clue, but the police brushed aside his advice. They were equally indifferent to his theory that the killer was a Starved Rock Lodge employee, especially since every worker there had been questioned to no avail.

The state police had spent a considerable time with one young employee on whose leather jacket a small spot of blood had been found, but when laboratory tests confirmed the suspect's claim that the stain was rabbit's blood, the investigators turned to other directions. Warren believed that they were too hasty, and at his insistence the man was subjected to not one but two lie detector tests, both of which brought definitely negative results.

Time slipped by, and at the end of four months the police admittedly were as far from a solution as when they had begun. Then, curiously, public opinion turned bitterly against Warren, although he had no responsibility for the investigation. He became the scapegoat instead of the police, with the newspapers accusing him of dereliction and failure. Nothing he could say in explanation of his duties and responsibility could assuage the mounting sentiment against him.

At last, however, he decided on a course of action. Although a lawyer, untrained in the ways of crime detection, he determined to launch an investigation of his own along lines that he believed the police had neglected. His first move was to ask the sheriff for help, and two reliable deputies were assigned to him.

These men, Wayne Hoss and William Bummett, had been engaged solely in civil affairs — both were as inexperienced as

Warren in detective work. But what they lacked was compensated for by their tenaciousness and dedication to justice. The three first turned their attention to the string, which Warren at the start had regarded as a vitally important clue.

Magnified many times until a single piece looked like a steel cable, Warren noted that it was made up of exactly twenty strands. His examination continued with every length of twine taken from the bodies. All were made up of the same number of fibres except for the last, which had only twelve. The prosecutor looked again and thought hard. Where had they come from and who had made them? Had they come from the lodge nearby? He wondered, and his speculation led him back to his original belief that the killer was a lodge employee.

He searched the place with his aides, picking up loose string in one room after another. After these finds had been carefully examined, a surprising fact came to light — every piece consisted of twenty strands excepting for two short lengths taken from the kitchen, each of which had only twelve. Warren went to the downtown retail store that supplied string to the lodge. There he learned the name of the factory, a plant in Marysville, Kentucky, and when Bummett and Hoss showed their samples from the hotel to the manufacturer, he quickly identified them as his product.

His prompt reply puzzled the investigators. "You seem so certain," Bummett remarked. "Aren't there other factories turning out the same kind of string?"

The manufacturer shook his head, explaining that his product was distinctive because of a peculiar dye that gave it a slightly different color. With this information, Warren decided on a daring move. Calling on the lodge management, he asked permission to have every employee tested by the lie detector, including as many former employees as could be located. The request was granted and the prosecutor, determined to call for the most experienced polygraph operator available, summoned John Reid of Chicago. In pursuing this course, he was acting on his suspicion that the test previously given to the young employee had not been intelligently handled.

Reid arrived on the scene with his equipment, set up a temporary working place near the lodge, and began the laborious task of testing one employee after another. Weeks passed without results; every test was negative.

Then a young man of twenty-one was brought before Reid in the course of his routine examinations. He said his name was Chester Weger, that he had once washed dishes at the lodge, but that he now supported his family as a house painter in a town some miles away.

He had no objection to the test, but before it was undertaken the detectives received a piece of information that caused them to wonder whether Reid would be wasting his time. Weger, they learned, was the man who had successfully passed two polygraph tests and satisfactorily explained the blood spot on his coat. Warren was consulted. "By all means let Reid test him," the prosecutor directed. "I know how Reid works — I know very little about the earlier operator."

Early the next afternoon Weger came into the improvised laboratory, seated himself casually, and joked with Reid as the lie detector straps were adjusted about his body. The test proceeded with the usual unrelated questions until at last Reid came abruptly and without warning to the first "dynamite question": "Why did you kill these women?"

"I didn't," the man in the chair answered, but at that instant the machine's recording needle leaped upward from its even course, reaching almost to the upper edge of the paper — a certain indication of lying. In view of what had happened twice before it was an incredible result.

As Reid and Warren discussed this dramatic turn, Reid explained that the accuracy of the polygraph depended entirely on expertise in its use, something that the prosecutor already recognized. They finally decided to subject Weger to still another test — the fourth. They told him that the equipment had not been properly adjusted, necessitating a "rerun." He laughed heartily, resumed his place, and the procedure was repeated — with the same result.

The conclusion, however, left Warren puzzled as to his next move. He knew of course that lie detector evidence was not admissible in court. Without it, he doubted that he had sufficient circumstantial evidence to convince a jury, and he finally concluded that his case was still too weak. Again his investigators went to work.

To their surprise they learned that Weger, who claimed that he had not been at the lodge at the time of the murders, had in fact been working there at that time. And when Weger's stained jacket was sent to the FBI laboratory, the technicians, resorting to recently developed tests, concluded that the red spot was in fact human blood. Still more incriminating evidence then came to light, including the statement of a former lodge guest who recognized a photograph of Weger as that of the man she had seen running from the murder scene.

At last the time had come to confront Weger with all this new evidence. Warren, hoping for a confession, was dubious but determined to try. He sent for the suspect and questioning began. An hour later extreme nervousness was apparent, and the prosecutor felt that a break was imminent. Relentlessly he pressed his queries with increasing sternness, until Weger began squirming in his chair. Moments later his head was in his hands.

"It's no use," he finally gasped. "I did it."

With tears trickling down his cheeks, Weger related all the ghastly details of the three murders. He said that being in debt, he had gone into the park intending to snatch a few purses from tourists. The three women were the first he encountered and to frighten them he picked up the tree bough.

Still bent only on robbery, he had bound two of the women with string taken from the lodge kitchen and was about to tie the third when one of the others wiggled free and hit him on the head with a pair of binoculars. He retaliated by knocking her unconscious with his club. It was then, in fear of capture, that he impulsively beat the three to death and dragged their bleeding bodies into the cave. He had pulled up their clothing, he admitted, to give the murders the appearance of a sex crime, hoping to throw the police off the track.

Warren and his aides had many questions to ask. Near the close of their long interrogation, Warren referred to the four lie detector tests, inquiring if Weger could explain how he had cheated the machine in the first two examinations.

The prisoner's face brightened. "It was easy," he replied smiling. "I filled myself up with aspirin and chased it down with Coke. It quiets a guy down, you know. Try it some time if you don't believe me."

On his twenty-second birthday Weger stood remorsefully in court and heard a jury pronounce him guilty. He was sentenced to life imprisonment.

A strange corollary to this case once occurred in an eastern penitentiary when an ignorant, superstitious prisoner inquired of his cellmates whether it were possible to fool the lie detector. They told him with straight faces that if he wore a small bottle filled with a certain liquid over his heart the machine could not record changes in heartbeats.

This he did but the examiner had been forewarned. After a number of simple questions, the prisoner finally was asked:

"Have you done anything to keep this test from working?"

"No," replied the surprised man, but despite the bottle the graph showed a sudden rise in pulse. Further tests convinced the authorities of his guilt.

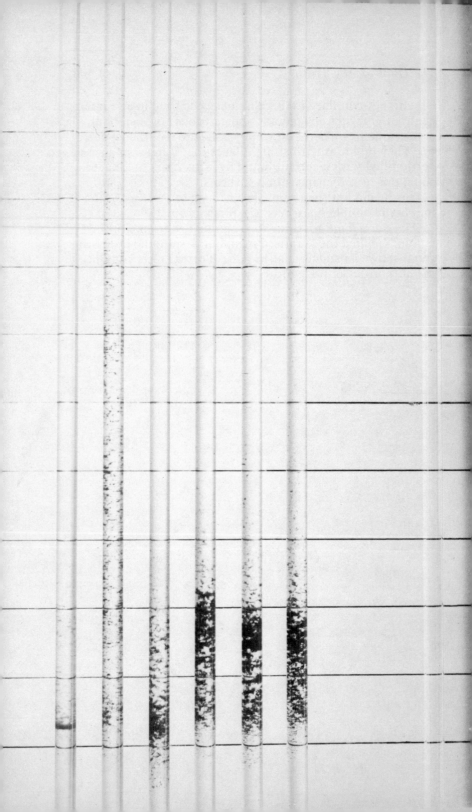

Chapter 13

Down to Earth

THE HISTORY OF scientific crime detection in the United States and abroad includes a number of dramatic cases in which unusually puzzling mysteries were solved by a few grains of earth that pointed an accusing finger and brought a murderer to bay.

In one such instance a prisoner was convicted through a bit of dust adhering to the wax in his ear. In another, the slayer of a woman whose body was found in New York's Central Park was found guilty with the help of a few particles of sand shaken from the cuffs of his trousers.

Much of the credit for the major advances in this field of inquiry belongs to Edmond Locard of the French Sûreté, Hans Gross, and Harry Soderman, the Swedish expert. Almost every authority, however, agrees that the original pioneer in this field was Sir Arthur Conan Doyle, who evidently was the first to realize the potential value of dirt and earth as clues and introduced them as the achievement of his fictional detective, Sherlock Holmes. Locard and the others were known to have been deeply impressed by Holmes's advanced thinking on the subject.

Conan Doyle is believed to have reached the conclusion that earth and dirt could provide useful clues while he was groping for a way to illustrate in fiction the importance of close observation and deduction. As he thought and wrote painstakingly, Conan Doyle discarded one idea after another until he suddenly hit upon what he was seeking. He decided to have his fictional detective demonstrate how a few particles of dirt on a man's shoe could provide detailed information on the wearer's movements.

The plot was intriguing and impressive, and Conan Doyle's *The Sign of Four* is still widely read; many letters reach Scot-

Soil under analysis

land Yard to this day addressed to Mr. Sherlock Holmes. What the author did not foresee, however, was that his imaginary situation would open the door to an entirely new area of laboratory work by criminalists, a technique that would serve the law through many years to come.

Conan Doyle's flight of fancy was as simple as it was ingenious. In conversation with his friend and roommate, Dr. Watson, Holmes casually remarks on a bit of reddish dirt clinging to the instep of the doctor's shoe. To the other's astonishment, Holmes observes wryly that his companion had been to the Wigmore Street post office that morning to dispatch a telegram. Then, with his characteristic smile, Holmes explained that dirt of that type and color obviously had come from a patch of ground at the entrance to the post office where the pavement had been torn up.

One of the many who read and enjoyed Conan Doyle's story was Edmond Locard, who died in 1951. For him the account of dirt on Dr. Watson's shoe was of great significance, and he berated himself for not having conceived the idea first. He was amazed that it could have come from a fiction writer rather than from someone professionally engaged in crime detection.

The more Locard thought about it, the more he realized that everybody comes into contact with particles of dust all the time and that this would certainly be true of an offender moving about the scene of his crime. He was encouraged further on reading a paper written by the famous Hans Gross, who not only supported the value of dust as a clue but recommended that the clothing worn by arrested suspects be beaten to extract any loose grains of dirt and grime.

Now fully confident of the importance of this new field, he confided his conclusions to his superiors, but they were not impressed. At first he lacked equipment, but he finally succeeded in obtaining adequate facilities to pursue his experiments.

Locard's new interest soon became an obsession. He continued to delve deeply into the subject, and in a few years he had collected and classified numerous types of dust and earth from vegetable, mineral, and animal sources. Then he set out to determine the state of these substances before they had become dust.

Others learned of what he was doing and turned to research

of their own, men like August Bruning of Berlin and Harry Soderman, who had discovered a valuable clue in a prisoner's car. Soderman, in his book, *Modern Criminal Investigation*, points to the need to always examine the dust on a prisoner's gloves. He cites a case in which the tiny glass particles found clinging to a burglar's gloves failed to match the window he was believed to have broken but finally led to the homes of his actual victims. However, it is to Locard that credit must be given for initiating this field of research. Jurgen Thorwald writes that Locard's research was a lasting contribution to criminology.

Locard's personal chagrin at his oversight in not realizing the importance of dirt as a clue before Conan Doyle moved him to write a scientific paper on the subject. Commenting on Holmes' ability to observe a spot of mud on Dr. Watson's shoe and to tell precisely what part of London the latter had recently visited, is cited as an outstanding achievement. He urged a careful and thoughtful reading of Conan Doyle's *A Study in Scarlet* and *The Sign of the Four* as illustrating his surprise at Conan Doyle's very early discovery of the value of dirt as evidence.

The results of Locard's studies had a major impact in the investigation of a mystery in the nation's capital in 1953. This was a case in which a small bagful of dust, sucked from the inside of an automobile by a vacuum cleaner, sent a murderer to the penitentiary. The discovery of the incriminating little particles was the climax of a long and unusual investigation directed by a shrewd detective determined to learn the truth. How he finally learned the truth with the help of dust and dirt provides one of the strangest chapters in the long history of the Metropolitan Police Department of Washington, D.C.

The crime came to light under peculiar circumstances late in the afternoon of Monday, September 8, 1958. The scene was a shallow section of the Anacostia River in the capital city. Three little boys were fishing when one of them engaged his hook in what appeared to be a large waterlogged bundle. As he tugged at his line with the help of his companions he saw to his horror that he was pulling in a human body.

Dropping their poles, the boys ran for help. A short time later the police were examining the remains of a young woman that appeared to have been submerged for some time. It was obvious that she had been murdered: a heavy slab of concrete was fastened to one leg with baling wire.

The body lacked any marks that might lead to identification, and while one squad of officers began a search of the area, another set out to ascertain the name of the victim. No one of her description had been reported missing, and the police could find no record of her fingerprints. Captain Lawrence A. Hartnett of the homicide squad had been placed in charge of the case, and at his direction descriptions of the murdered woman were broadcast over police and private radio stations. Before long he learned from the coroner that the victim had been strangled before her weighted body had been thrown into the water.

Her identity was established two days later, when the manager of a government building noted her absence from the switchboard where she had worked. As she was known for her punctual habits, he became alarmed, and a co-worker to whom he had made inquiries called his attention to the newspaper accounts of the unidentified body. A visit to the morgue confirmed his fears. The victim was Mrs. Ruth Reeves, a prepossessing young woman in her early thirties.

Captain Hartnett was alerted and hurried to the woman's apartment, which he found listed in the telephone book. Suspecting that she might have been killed in her home and her body moved to the river, he was surprised to find the apartment in perfect order with no sign of trouble. Neighbors said that Mrs. Reeves, being separated from her husband, lived alone but often received male friends. They had last seen her two days before when she left home presumably for work. Her car was still parked outside.

Hartnett thoroughly examined the rooms and was attracted by a photograph of the murdered woman with a man of good appearance. He showed it to one of the neighbors who recognized the man as "Phil," an erstwhile friend of Mrs. Reeves, and though the informant did not know his last name, she had been told that he was employed by the housing authority.

"What do you know about this man Phil?" Hartnett inquired of the neighbor.

"Not much," he was told. "But I do know that he was extremely jealous when she parted company with him; in fact some time ago he threatened to kill her."

Hartnett, accompanied by Detective George Donahue, set out for the housing offices. They soon learned that the man they wanted to meet was Philmore Clarke, about forty years of age, a long-time and highly respected employee. He had left on vacation two days before the body had been found and was believed to have driven out of the city in a hardtop Oldsmobile loaned to him by a woman friend.

Their next move was to visit his home. There his son confirmed that Clarke was away on vacation and had not stated when he would return. Before the officers left, however, their suspicions were aroused by something they observed: they noted that the front garden was enclosed by a row of concrete blocks resembling the one tied to the body. Two were missing. Moreover, they noticed a coil of wire in a rear hall that looked very much like the wire fastened to the murder victim's leg.

Both detectives regarded these finds as significant but agreed that it was too soon to guess at conclusions. Two men in plain clothes were posted close to the house to await Clarke's return, especially since it had been learned that he was still in the city.

The watch came to a sudden end two days later when Clarke was arrested while approaching the house. Questioned for hours, he denied any knowledge of the murder, explaining that he had last seen Mrs. Reeves on Sunday morning, a day before the body was recovered. She was in good health, he said, appeared to be happy, and they had parted on friendly terms.

Clarke appeared to be unconcerned when asked about the missing concrete blocks. Somewhat evasive, he suggested that Mrs. Reeves probably had been killed by her new boyfriend who might have taken the concrete from Clarke's place to throw suspicion on him. Asked about the car he had been seen driving, he told the officers that it had been loaned to him and had been stolen while parked outside a friend's home.

Judging by Clarke's manner and his attempts to dismiss questions about the cement, Hartnett now reasoned that his prisoner was either guilty or at least knew far more than he chose to tell. How to prove these suspicions was another matter. The missing car, he believed, might provide an important clue. A detailed description of the Oldsmobile was broadcast by radio and teletype; its license number, more recently learned, was listed.

As the search continued, Hartnett decided that the time had come to call on the FBI crime laboratory for assistance. Its technicians were asked to compare the concrete slab tied to the body with those in Clarke's garden. The wire from his home would be studied side by side with that taken from the water. Several days were spent in intensive scientific study, and when the laboratory men finally reported the detective learned that the tests had further confirmed his suspicions.

In spite of this Hartnett and his colleagues realized that they still faced serious problems. Clarke had already been charged with murder, but the officers felt that their evidence, completely circumstantial, would be insufficient to convince a jury. Their last hope was pinned to the missing car and what it might disclose. It was recovered days later not far from Clarke's home, and the police were certain that it had been hidden by friends of Clarke.

Hartnett's orders to his associates were now specific and direct. "I'm certain that there's damaging evidence in that car," he told them. "I want every inch of it examined; pull the upholstery apart and use a vacuum cleaner to get out every grain of dust you can find. If this fails our case is lost."

A full day was spent in scrutinizing the car inside and out, until Hartnett had a bag bulging with dust and dirt ready for laboratory study. He could scarcely wait for a report, and when it came he believed that his problems were nearly over. The laboratory technicians, analyzing the dust chemically and studying it under the microscope, had found specks of a strange black silica slag of a sort they had never seen before. Particles of the same peculiar substance had been found imbedded in Clarke's clothing and in the seams of the dead woman's garments.

"Where could all this slag have come from?" Hartnett asked himself, knowing that he must find the answer. If he could do that he might be able to complete his case by definitely establishing Clarke's presence at the spot where the body was found.

After some thinking he turned to one of his men. "The time has come," he said, "for me to do some old-fashioned digging — and I mean that literally. Get me a couple of shovels and a pair of overalls. I intend to do it myself."

With his equipment in the back of the car, the detective

drove to the exact place where the body had been found. It did not take him long to fill a small bag with dirt. Then he moved a short distance away and filled a second bag with grime from the surface of the roadway. Both specimens were rushed to the laboratory.

In the first sack the experts found the same type of black slag particles detected in the car dust and in the clothing. No such substance could be detected in the second bag. Hartnett's key question still remained unanswered, but one of the FBI men had a suggestion. "This type of silica slag comes from an industrial furnace," he advised. "Is there one anywhere in the area where you were working?"

Hartnett soon learned that such a furnace was operated a few miles from the river by an electric power concern. A sample of its slag was analyzed; it was identical to that already studied.

"What becomes of this slag?" Hartnett inquired eagerly of the foreman. "Just how do you get rid of it?"

"We get a trucking company to cart it away," the foreman replied. "Why don't you talk to them?"

The detective followed that advice and received the answer to his vital question. He was told that a considerable quantity of the slag had been dumped over a single block of roadway for city authorities who wished to test its value as a surfacing material. That lone block was only a few feet from where the body of Mrs. Reeves had been found.

"And what do you do with the rest of the stuff you haul away?" the captain inquired, eager to reassure himself.

The power plant foreman pointed ahead of him. "We dump it on private property in that direction," he explained. "We have a permit from a private property owner."

The district attorney, with the evidence provided by the police, was now ready to bring Clarke before a jury. First, however, he wanted to try for a confession, but the accused man clung to his plea of innocence and boasted that he would be quickly acquitted.

December 9 was set as the day for the trial. In the meantime Clarke and his counsel evidently learned something of the state's case, for a series of delays on technical grounds came to a sudden end. That morning Clarke appeared before Judge J. Sirica and pleaded guilty.

Questioned by the court, he admitted killing Mrs. Reeves in her own apartment after a bitter quarrel over her affections and hauling her body, after it had been weighted, to the river. A few days later he received an indeterminate penitentiary sentence of from five to twenty-five years.

In much the same way New York police and their laboratory experts once succeeded in sending a wife killer to the electric chair. His name was Anibal Almondover. A little soil, no more than a thimbleful taken from his trousers cuff, proved his undoing.

The body of the victim, Mrs. Louise Almondover, was found hidden in an unfrequented part of Central Park on a cloudy day in November 1942. Careful examination by the autopsy surgeon convinced him that she had been the victim of a strangler and that death had occurred twenty-four hours earlier. The location of the remains convinced police that the woman had been killed elsewhere and her body dragged to where it was found.

In their scrupulous search for clues detectives turned to the young woman's husband, from whom she had been estranged for months, but his eagerness to clear himself convinced them that he probably knew far more than he was telling. Claiming an airtight alibi, he asserted that he had been to a dance the night of the murder, his companion being a girl of whom his wife had been extremely jealous.

This young woman's story corroborated what Almondover had said, and others who had attended the dance told of having seen the couple together. Though this information tended to confirm the husband's alibi, the officers were still not fully convinced, and they decided to detain him pending further inquiry.

The following day they learned that Almondover had pawned the clothing he had worn on the night of the murder. They were certain that he would not have left evidence in his pockets, but the possibility of dust interested them, for they had studied Locard's original experiments and their development.

The pawned garments were recovered and turned over to the laboratory. Inch by inch they were examined under the microscope and for some time nothing of importance was found.

However, when the technicians turned down the trousers cuffs they were rewarded. Adhering to the cloth were a few particles of dust and grime. While this was being scrutinized, a man was dispatched to the exact spot in Central Park where the body had been found with instructions to bring back a sample of earth. The specimens proved to be precisely alike.

Still the laboratory men were unwilling to announce a definite conclusion. Samples of park dirt within ten, fifteen, and twenty feet of the vital area were obtained. They were different from the specimens taken from the trousers. Only then did the technicians announce their findings as positive.

Almondover was charged with murder and told that his guilt had been proven. Minutes later he said that he was ready to confess. He said that he had been walking through the park with his estranged wife, that the story of the dance was a hoax, and that he had persuaded his friends to corroborate it.

His confession was front page news, but on second thought he decided against going to the electric chair without a legal struggle. He hired an attorney who decided to challenge the findings of the state's experts. To everyone's surprise Almondover stood before the court a few days later and pleaded not guilty.

The trial was brief. Appearing for the state were the laboratory men, who explained in detail how they had reached their conclusions. This, as was expected, was attacked by the defense counsel, but the jurors had been thoroughly impressed by the prosecution witnesses. The defendant was convicted of murder and sentenced to death in New York' Sing Sing Prison.

Chapter 14

Clues Are Everywhere

THANKS TO ADVANCES made by scientists in the crime laboratory, most substances, organic or inorganic, can be made to speak accusing or exonerating words under special circumstances, given, of course, the proper technical study. Wood is one; sawdust, ashes, and even bits of metal are others. In a different field, tire marks have proved to be of great importance.

In their attempts to link housebreakers with a specific crime, technicians often succeed in obtaining damning evidence from a tiny particle of wood adhering to a jimmy, a chisel, or a hammer used to force open a door or window. In examining shavings and sawdust retrieved from holes bored in desks and table drawers, laboratory men often get significant help from a few grains of varnish or paint that reveal their nature when properly tested. A xylotomist — as an authority on wood and its composition is called — can determine from a chip what type of tree it has come from.

America's classic example of the value of wood analysis comes from the trial and conviction of Bruno Hauptmann, the kidnapper and killer of the infant son of Colonel Charles A. Lindbergh in 1932. Aside from other less important circumstantial evidence, Hauptmann's guilt was established through the technical skill of Arthur Koehler, who served for many years as the government's chief expert on woods under the jurisdiction of the United States Forest Service.

Koehler undertook his difficult and highly specialized task months after the police had exhausted a maze of conflicting clues, their work made even more confusing by offers from mysterious individuals to contact the kidnapper with ransom money. The homemade ladder, which the kidnapper had used to reach a window of the Lindbergh nursery, had been elimi-

Wood — what is its source?

nated as a clue when it failed to reveal a single fingerprint. Only then did Koehler enter the case, but he did so with a brilliant record of earlier accomplishments in other cases.

Years before he had brought a bomber to justice by first identifying a small remnant of his device as elm wood and then matching it with pieces of the same kind of lumber in the suspect's possession. In another mystery he obtained the confession of an arsonist by demonstrating the precise similarity between a charred stick in the debris of a demolished home and a plank in the owner's toolhouse.

With this kind of experience in determining the composition of different kinds of wood, Koehler was the logical man to undertake a solution of the Lindbergh mystery by studying the ladder. In Trenton, New Jersey, where this neglected piece of evidence had been impounded by the state police, he went to work after forewarning the authorities that they were not to expect any report for a considerable time. With a microscope and other necessary scientific equipment, he undertook to scrutinize every inch of the ladder, to make a witness of every rung.

First he disassembled it, carefully marking every piece so that its place could be easily recalled. Before long, he knew that the ladder was made up of three sections and that different kinds of wood had been used by its maker, principally pine and fir, but of different varieties that came from different areas. He also studied the plane markings on the rungs, which indicated the use of more than one kind of tool. The growth rings on the various woods disclosed the ages of the pieces.

After months of further painstaking work, which no one but an unusually skilled specialist could have performed, Koehler finally decided to concentrate his efforts on one particular rung, which he believed could be most readily identified by lumber experts on the basis of its distinctive material and planing. He selected a rung that he thought had come from a mill on the Atlantic seaboard, but because there were hundreds in that locality, how to find the right place was a challenging task.

Nevertheless he finally traced the wood to a South Carolina mill, but even then only half his work was done. He had to learn the name of the lumberyard to which this particular type of board with the distinctive kind of planing had been shipped.

Almost a year of persistent search had passed when Koehler, visiting a lumberyard in an outer part of New York City, suddenly came upon the exact piece of lumber for which he had been hunting. It was obvious that whoever had purchased similar wood must live close by.

By clever detective work the purchase of this particular planking was traced to Hauptmann. The rest of the story is history. Koehler's expertise in his field and his tenaciousness had solved one of the most baffling crimes of the century.

Late in 1953 five tiny pieces of metal, in the competent hands of FBI laboratory technicians, solved one of the most ghastly air disasters of all time and led to the execution of a man who murdered forty-four people, including his own mother.

The crash occurred in the early morning of November 1, 1953 when a crowded United Airlines plane crashed in flames on a farm near Longmont, Colorado. It had taken off only eleven minutes before from Stapleton Airport in Denver bound for Seattle, Washington. Bodies and debris were scattered over a mile and a half.

The first task, of course, involved identification of the victims; the next was to determine the cause of the tragedy, to learn whether malfunction of the aircraft or some diabolical plot was responsible. FBI experts arrived on the scene, ready to assist the officials of the airline and representatives of the Civil Aeronautics Board.

Even before the search for bodies had been concluded, the men from the FBI prepared to follow their customary procedure in such cases — the construction of a mock-up of the ill-fated craft. (This is done by attaching a wire mesh "skin" to a sturdily built wooden frame resembling the skeleton of the plane. Into this can be placed every little one of the thousands of fragments picked up at the scene of the crash.)

The task, continuing for weeks, disclosed that the tail section of the plane had been severed from the fuselage and had hit the ground a mile and a half from where the nose section and engines had been found almost intact. When further study failed to attribute the explosion to a malfunction of the aircraft, only two explanations remained — either one of the pilots had erred or the disaster was due to a murderous plot.

The investigators looked hopefully to the mock-up for a clue. After much work each fragment of wreckage had been recovered, fitted into the dummied frame of the aircraft, marked for the identification of their exact location, and finally moved carefully to a large, guarded warehouse.

By this meticulous procedure, the experts found that the explosion had taken place in the rear cargo pit, known technically as station 718, situated directly across from the cargo compartment. They verified this conclusion by finding that the strips of the heavy fuselage skin that fitted into this section had been torn to shreds. There was still further evidence to support this belief. So great had been the force of the blast at this point that small pieces of wreckage had been found in shoes taken from luggage known to have been stored in this cargo section.

This led to a thorough checking of the cargo shipments, but when it was learned that nothing of an inflammable nature had been stored in the area under suspicion, the experts found themselves obliged to turn to other directions. Above all, they agreed, the mock-up should be continued with all possible speed.

At its conclusion, one of the FBI experts came forward with significant news. In the presence of a group of others directing the inquiry, he took from his pocket a small plastic envelope and emptied it on a table. Before him lay five little pieces of sheet metal, none larger than a fifty-cent piece.

"These tiny bits," he began, "are in my judgment the key to the solution. They are the only fragments that we absolutely cannot fit into the mock-up. They simply do not belong either to the plane or to what we know of the cargo."

The scraps were scrutinized and found to be badly burned; moreover, they were covered with a deposit of soot like the residue of an explosion. On further examination, one of the men looked through his pocket glass and observed that one of the fragments bore the letters HO in red.

"Could the answer be a bomb?" someone inquired. The others nodded. FBI chemists were summoned, and the little metal pieces were subjected to tests — with significant results. They produced evidence of sodium carbonate, nitrate, and sulphur compounds, which are common to nitroglycerin from which dynamite is made.

It was now apparent that the plane had been blown up with dynamite, but where it was obtained and how it was carried into the fuselage remained to be determined. The next step called for an explanation of the cryptic letters, HO, and an answer was soon forthcoming. The fragment so marked had been part of a battery of the type used to set off a bomb!

This necessitated an inquiry into each of the forty-four men and women aboard the plane, his or her background, and the kind of hand luggage carried aboard. The investigators were also obliged to make every effort to match portions of luggage taken from the debris with that known to have been in the possession of each passenger.

The work was progressing slowly when the FBI men suddenly uncovered what appeared to be a clue of major importance. They came across the name of a woman passenger, Mrs. Daisie King of Denver. Many of her effects, including newspaper clippings and a checkbook, had been found in the debris. The clippings involved her son, Jack Gilbert Graham, and his reported trouble over a check. This disclosure obviously aroused suspicion over his integrity.

Graham at once became a suspect, and it was soon learned that shortly before his mother's departure on the plane, three insurance policies on her life had been purchased with Jack Graham as the sole beneficiary. The inquiry now turned on Graham and his past. It was revealed that he lived a rather unsavory life and that a restaurant he had once owned had been demolished by a mysterious explosion.

The time to question Graham had come, but he denied any responsibility for the fatal plane crash, insisting that he was innocent of wrongdoing. His wife, however, unintentionally added to the suspicions of the investigators when she disclosed that her husband had packed his mother's suitcase and, at the last moment, had included what she had been told was a "surprise gift." A search of his home uncovered a coil of insulated copper wire used in detonating caps and the policies insuring his mother's life.

Under severe grilling, he gradually weakened and finally confessed his guilt, relating how he had made the bomb and hidden it in his mother's suitcase.

Convicted of first-degree murder, he paid with his life in the gas chamber of the Colorado State Penitentiary. Five little

pieces of metal, picked up in the debris of the wrecked plane —
the fragments that would not fit into the mock-up — had
revealed his bizarre plot.

The use of tire marks in criminal investigation dates back
to the early years of the twentieth century when automobiles
first came into use. Credit for the first experiments in this
direction goes to Harry Soderman of Sweden and a Frenchman
named Chavigny. But not until 1931 did this procedure come
into fully acceptable use in crime laboratories.

As the years passed, however, new systems were devised to
include the steadily increasing numbers of automobile tires
and their widely differing patterns. They are now divided into
two classifications — symmetrical and asymmetrical. In each
category there are many subdivisions to facilitate efforts to
link an imprint in the dust with the tire that made it. But many
obstacles often present themselves. On many tires the tread
has been so worn that the pattern is not discernible, and on
some cars there is a different pattern on each tire.

Tire marks are of special value in the investigation of hit-
and-run cases where they frequently point to a guilty driver.
Yet they have often played important roles in investigating
murders, burglaries, and other types of crimes.

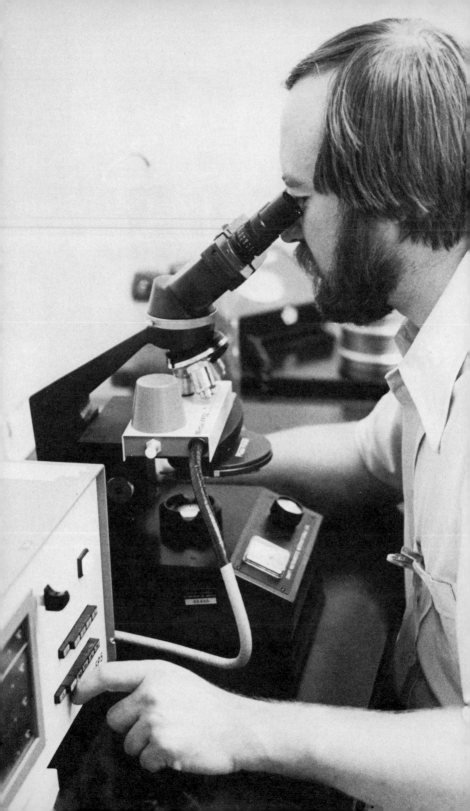

Chapter 15

Splinters of Glass

VISITORS TOURING THE MASSIVE building housing the Federal Bureau of Investigation in Washington, D.C. frequently linger before the large glassed entrance to one of the laboratories, bewildered and fascinated by what they see. While each of the many workrooms has its own attractions, this one appears to draw more curiosity and interest than any other.

Inside are white-gowned men and women bending intently over large metal trays filled with little particles of broken glass. Using long, slim metal rods and sometimes forceps, they poke among the fragments as if looking for something they cannot find. Occasionally a worker will stop abruptly, pick up a shiny bit of glass no larger than a diamond, step to a strange looking instrument, and gaze at his find as though he had suddenly come upon a gem of fabulous value.

"What in the world are these people doing?" someone inquires of the guide.

"Just what you see," he answers smiling. "They are looking for clues in tiny particles of broken glass."

"But clues to what?"

"To hit-and-run cases, to murders, to robberies, and many other crimes."

The fragments, he goes on to explain, have been sent to the laboratory in the hope that they will disclose valuable evidence. Some have been picked up at the scenes of accidents or of homicides, others have been taken from the clothing or even the hair of a victim or a suspect.

While laboratory facilities and equipment for glass examination are available in all state police centers and in most of the larger cities, the resources of the FBI in this area are recognized as the largest and best in the country. That is why the mail delivered each day to the FBI includes many little packages of

Analysis of glass particles under a specialized microscope

glass fragments with explanations of their significance and requests for examination.

Today's techniques in this intricate and specialized field are the result of many years of study and experimentation, for at one time glass comparisons could be made only by visual examination, which in many cases relied largely on guess-work. But as far back as the 1880s a skillful investigator in an eastern city of the United States used a small splinter of glass to convict a man of murder. The case at first appeared to involve only the burglary of a jewelry store, but it assumed far more serious proportions when the murdered body of the owner was found in a back room close to a broken window.

A suspect was arrested in his hotel room, and a search of his suitcase disclosed a small piece of glass no larger than a dime. "That came from the top of a soda bottle I broke trying to open it," said the suspect; the police were not so certain. The splinter was taken to a laboratory and compared with glass from the shattered pane. They were found to be identical and the suspect confessed.

Steady advances, however, have now made it possible to determine with unerring accuracy when a piece of glass has come from a certain window, an automobile headlight, a bottle, or some other source. The importance of this progress is clearly recognized by criminalists for, as Lewis G. Mickells, a Scotland Yard authority, once said, "The substance of great-est interest among manufactured materials in the investigation of crime is glass."

The modern laboratory technician usually begins with a pre-liminary, wholly nontechnical examination of the specimens to determine such easily distinguished variables as thickness, color, and surface characteristics. The next process is the com-parative study of density or specific gravity, which is deter-mined by immersing the glass fragment in a beaker or test tube containing a salt or mercury solution. By measuring with a micrometer the point at which the inserted object neither sinks nor floats, the specific gravity is determined.

Experts also have at their disposal two further procedures for checking. One is known as the refractive index, which tells the relative velocity of light through the glass, and the third is called optical dispersion, a means of accurately measuring the width of the band of colors that can be seen when a beam of light passes through the glass. These are routine methods of correctly ascertaining whether two little pieces of glass have come from the same source, a determination that can mean freedom or prison for a person accused of crime.

Aside from this particular area of research, however, there is often another challenge facing experts who work with glass. They may be called on to pass judgment on bullet holes in windows — of either homes or cars — determining from which direction the projectile has come — from the inside or the outside. Such a decision can obviously be of major importance in an investigation.

Harry Soderman presents the issue clearly in his book *Modern Criminal Investigation*. He points out that a bullet with a strong charge makes a hole with the sharpest edges and that a bullet traveling a long distance will fracture the glass in the same way as a stone. Explaining the method for determining the direction of the shot, he states that the glass flakes will have been blown away on only one side of the hole indicating that the bullet came from the opposite surface of the opening with the missing flakes.

An FBI expert, writing on a subject a few years ago in the Bureau's monthly bulletin, attacked the viewpoint that the side from which glass fragments fall indicates the side from which the force was applied. This, he contended, was not always true and might well lead to incorrect conclusions. He explained that when a window is struck, glass, being flexible, bends in the direction of the blow and causes the opposite side to be stretched. The tension so produced results in cracks that radiate out from the point of impact, like the spokes of a wheel.

An instruction sheet, distributed recently to students in a criminalistics class in a western university, presented these interesting observations in the study of glass fractures:

When the edges of a piece of broken glass are examined closely, a number of curved lines, called stress lines, may be observed. Stress lines will run at an acute angle almost parallel to one side of the glass and curve to meet the other side perpendicularly. Stress lines are always perpendicular to the side that broke first.

When there is more than one bullet hole in a pane of glass, it is possible to determine which was made first. A fracture in glass may travel some distance, but if it meets another fracture it stops. . . .

Fragments of glass and interpretation of glass fractures have proved of great value in criminal investigations and provided convincing evidence at trials.

Some years ago, bullet holes in the car windows of two
notorious fugitives assumed paramount importance to the FBI
at the height of a long and relentless pursuit of one of the
country's most desperate gangsters, "Baby Face" Nelson,
whose real name was Lester Joseph Gillis. He was wanted for
many crimes, including the cold-blooded killing of W. Carter
Baum, a former G-man, in a western town on April 22, 1934.

Spurred into even greater activity by the Baum murder, the
FBI learned that Gillis's companion at that time had been John
Paul Chase, a man of many aliases who was high on the "most
wanted" list; both men were members of the infamous Dil-
linger gang. These two men and their associates, operating
boldly in various parts of the country, were well-known in law
enforcement circles. Chase had first run afoul of the law as a
bootlegger near San Francisco and once had escaped from
Illinois State Penitentiary while serving time for bank robbery.

The encounter that ended in their downfall arose from information reaching the FBI that Chase and Gillis, sneaking into
the outskirts of Chicago, had stolen a Ford V-8 sedan into
which they had loaded guns, ammunition, and bulletproof
vests hastily unpacked from their pickup truck abandoned
close by. With Gillis at the wheel and Chase in the rear seat,
the two had then driven to the home of a friend in Wisconsin.
From there they were seen moving in the direction of Lake
Geneva in the same state, traveling along the Northwest
Highway.

By this time, FBI agent Samuel P. Cowley had planned a
trap. Calling on other agents to hasten to an arranged rendezvous, Cowley started out for the meeting place with agent H. E.
Hollis, expecting to join his other colleagues before encounter-
ing their quarry. Before their arrival, however, three other
agents in a Ford coupe, responding to Cowley's summons,
suddenly sighted a sedan resembling the car stolen by the
fugitives. The last three digits of its license number, 578,
corresponded with the number of the wanted machine —
639-578.

The G-men quickly swerved their car to ascertain the complete license number and saw the sedan turn the other way, its fleeing occupants knowing that they had been seen. There was more swift maneuvering by both cars. The sedan license number had been verified, and the agents realized that a clash was imminent.

Minutes later Gillis, by a deft turn, brought his car directly behind that of his pursuers. Chase, leaning forward from his rear seat, raised his automatic rifle and took quick aim at the agents' vehicle. Five shots rang out in quick succession, plowing through the windshield of the FBI car. The battle was on! In a flash, one of the agents drew his revolver and returned the fire, shooting through the rear glass of his car.

At that moment Cowley and Hollis suddenly approached in a four-door Hudson, having heard the shooting and realizing what was taking place. Determined to capture the gangsters regardless of the danger to themselves, they swung around, heading for the wanted men. The pursuit had barely started when the fugitives' car came to a sudden halt with steaming water spouting from its radiator, hit by a bullet during the fusillade.

Chase and Gillis leaped to the ground and turned their machine gun on their pursuers. Above the crackling of shots came a cry of pain. Moments later all was silent.

Agents Cowley and Hollis were dead. The two fugitives had disappeared. Not until the following day was Gillis' riddled body found some distance away in a clump of shrubbery.

The hunt for Chase continued, and FBI men picked up his trail leading westward. Following one clue after another they finally captured him at Shasta in northern California, hundreds of miles away from the scene of the battle.

Preposterous as it may seem, Chase immediately assumed an air of injured innocence, insisting that he was not guilty of murder. He claimed that he and Gillis had been fired on first by the agents without provocation and that he and Gillis had returned the fire in self-defense. He further asserted that the agents' bullets had entered their rear window.

Chase engaged lawyers who boasted that they could support his defense in court. However, they did not know what FBI technicians were doing with shattered glass at the crime laboratory in Washington. The machine occupied by the gangsters had been recovered and taken to FBI headquarters.

There a carefully selected group of glass specialists had been assigned to undertake an exhaustive study of the car's windshield and rear window.

Following customary procedures, they set out to ascertain the direction of the bullets that had penetrated the glass. Had they come from the outside — in this case from the agents' guns — or from the inside of the gangsters' car? Utilizing the various laboratory tests, they finally reported that the bullet holes in the fugitives' car could only have come from the *inside*, fired by Chase and Gillis. Science had thoroughly refuted the plea of self-defense.

These results, of course, were not known to the defense when the trial opened in Chicago. Chase's lawyers had told newsmen to wait for a surprise; they were confident of proving, they said, that their client was not guilty of murdering the two agents despite his long criminal record.

But Chase and his attorneys were due for an unexpected surprise. They listened in amazement as one after another of the FBI experts took the stand to explain in minute detail how they had studied the splintered windows of the accused man's car and determined by technical methods that the bullet holes had come only from his weapon and that of his dead companion.

The defense witnesses made no impact in trying to discredit this testimony. Chase was found guilty of murder and sentenced to life imprisonment.

Sometimes in cases that include strongly incriminating findings, the accused will plead guilty, saving the state the time and expense involved in trials. So it was in two relatively recent cases told to me by Dr. Lowell W. Bradford, chief of the Laboratory of Criminalistics of California's Santa Clara County, which demonstrate the increasing use of glass splinters in day-to-day police work everywhere.

In one case nineteen-year-old Edward Lee Davis went to jail because he did not know that a speck of glass from a shattered window had imbedded itself in the nonskid pattern of his rubber-soled tennis shoes.

On a warm June night in California's "garden city," San Jose, a crash of glass attracted a patrolman to a large farm machinery plant in an industrial district. A number of burglaries in recent nights had caused all patrolmen to be on the lookout for a youth driving a sedan. Reaching the factory, the officer found that the burglar had entered by smashing a large window leading to a restroom. The office was in disarray, and it was apparent that a considerable amount of equipment had been taken.

The patrolman who had signaled for help was soon joined by other officers. Searching the neighborhood, they observed a car parked in a dark alley. The youthful driver identified himself as Davis and denied any knowledge of the burglary, although a typewriter and other office equipment were piled on the back seat.

At headquarters he was subjected to a careful search, which yielded nothing until he was told to remove his shoes. It was then that a piece of glass was found imbedded in the sole of his right shoe; this was turned over to Dr. Bradford with other small glass fragments picked up on the floor beside the shattered window.

Bradford and his aides went to work with their specimens, checking them for specific gravity and refractive index in the manner already described. Their report stated unequivocally that the fragment from the prisoner's shoe was exactly the same as the splinters from the window. Through the prison grapevine Davis learned of the laboratory report and realizing his predicament, pleaded guilty. He was sentenced to six months in the county jail.

Palo Alto, seat of Stanford University, eighteen miles north of San Jose, was the scene of the other crime reported by Dr. Bradford. Though circumstances differed, the result was the same.

Shortly before four o'clock on a February morning, police responded to a burglar alarm from a downtown sporting goods store and arrived just in time to see two poorly dressed boys speeding away in a dilapidated machine. The officers gave chase and the police car, with its siren screeching, zigzagged through the dark downtown streets for many blocks until the fugitives were finally forced to the curb and captured. They gave their names as William Gipsom and Lenzo V. Young, aged nineteen and twenty years respectively.

Examination of the runaway machine disclosed several tiny pieces of glass adhering to the bumper and fender area. Pressed for an explanation, the two young prisoners had little to say, merely suggesting that someone must have backed into their machine while parking.

Police learned differently, however, when they returned to the store and discovered that someone had forced an entry by ramming a car against a rear door. A considerable amount of shattered glass lay on the ground, both inside and outside the splintered door. The laboratory tests were the same as in the San Jose burglary except that in addition to comparing the specific gravity and refractive index, the color and thickness of the glass in evidence were identical.

Gipsom and Young both pleaded guilty.

Chapter 16
Telltale Voices

O N MAY 26, 1965, sixty-five years after Scotland Yard first introduced fingerprinting, an American soldier was found guilty by a new form of evidence, voiceprints — a graphic pattern of the human voice said to be as accurate a means of identification as the mark of a fingertip. An invention of the present decade, voiceprints are considered by many to be the last word in modern crime detection techniques.

The defendant in this history-making case was James C. Wright, attached to a United States Air Force base in California. On the visual evidence of a weird-looking pattern of lines produced electronically from a tape recording of his voice, a court-martial of eleven officers agreed that beyond doubt Wright was guilty of making anonymous obscene telephone calls to hostesses at the base hospital.

The graph was interpreted before the military court by the inventor of voiceprints, tall, fifty-nine-year-old Dr. Lawrence G. Kersta of Somerville, New Jersey, a widely known electronic scientist who is now being called "America's sound sleuth."

Facing the air force court as an expert witness, Dr. Kersta exhibited a number of strange-looking spectographs on paper, which he explained had been made from tape recordings of the voice that had repeatedly made insulting remarks to the hostesses. The voiceprint machine, he stated, tunes in on each frequency of a sound in the same way that a radio listener tunes in on one station after another, except that in the case of the voiceprinter the tuning is done by a magnetic head that moves back and forth across a strip of tape.

"Voiceprints," he declared, "are as reliable as fingerprints in establishing the identity of a person. No two human voices are the same in every respect, and the equipment I use can

Voice prints being recorded on a spinning drum

detect any attempt to disguise a voice, even if someone tries to speak with a mouthful of marbles or overindulges in liquor."

Noting curious expressions on the faces of some of his listeners, he proceeded to expound some elementary principles. "When children first learn to speak," he went on, "they discover their own way of using their vocal apparatus, which includes not only the vocal cords but the throat, mouth, nose, sinuses, lips, teeth, tongue, soft palate, and jaw muscles. So you see that the way children combine all these factors causes their simplest words to be uttered with a combination of sound wave frequencies that are unlike the same word spoken by any other person. We can use voiceprints to detect differences that are not audible to the human ear. And remember," he added with a smile, "you can't fingerprint an obscene or threatening telephone call."

Dr. Kersta, who proudly asserts that voiceprints have vindicated innocent people as well as established the guilt of others, began his initial experiments on the development of the system in 1961 while on the staff of the Bell Telephone Laboratories as a scientist in the department of speech. He had joined the staff at the age of nineteen. His first success was presented to the Acoustical Society of America in May 1962, and accounts of continuing progress were made in papers read to various other American scientific bodies.

"The first law enforcement application of voiceprints," he has told me, "was conducted while I was still at the Bell Laboratories and was performed for the Connecticut State Police. We proved that a person held on suspicion of making bodily harm threats to a Connecticut state official was innocent. Our cooperation resulted in the arrest of the real culprit."

One of the most recent uses of voiceprints resulted in the quick conviction of a man arrested on charges of telephoning a bomb threat to the headquarters of the Orlando Police Department in Florida — the first time that the electronic system was used in that state.

When the unidentified caller's menacing message reached the police, officers quickly adjusted their tape recorder and obtained an almost complete reproduction of the conversation. Investigation pointed suspiciously at twenty-seven-year-old Joseph Worley, who was taken into custody despite his protests. "I didn't get to make any call," he insisted. "I was in a phone booth trying to call my buddy, but I couldn't get him on the line because his phone was out of order and my dime kept coming back."

The police, however, thought differently. When Worley came into court a few days later two voiceprint experts testified that a spectograph made of the tape recording had proven conclusively that the threatening voice was the defendant's. One expert, Dr. Oscar Tosi of Washington State University, told the jury that the percentage of error in voiceprint identification was negligible. He said that he based this conclusion on a ten-year study.

The other state witness was Detective Sergeant Ernest Nash of the Michigan State Police, who first stated that he believed voiceprints to be as highly reliable as fingerprints. He then related how he had compared the voice of the person making the bomb threat with a recording of Worley's voice.

"Now tell the jury," asked County Solicitor Ron Powell, "what the spectograph patterns of both recorded voiceprints showed."

"They showed the two voices to be precisely the same," Nash replied without hesitation. "Neither could be the voice of anyone else but the defendant."

It took the jury only fifteen minutes to reach a verdict finding Worley guilty. Powell, the prosecutor, was surrounded by newsmen as he left the courtroom. Asked for comment, he stated, "I feel that the verdict makes a significant event for law enforcement in Florida."

In a case more than a year earlier in New Brunswick, New Jersey, voiceprints opened prison doors for John W. Krapp, a twenty-seven-year-old special policeman who had already been convicted of making a long series of annoying telephone calls to a former fellow-worker, Walter Bohlen, who testified that he was certain he could recognize Krapp's voice. The calls, he explained, occurred while both men were working for the same company, and Bohlen had assumed that Krapp was resentful because Bohlen had replaced him on a job.

Krapp, insisting that he had been wrongly accused, appealed his conviction, a move that brought S. Philip Klein into the case as the prosecutor. After studying the testimony of the earlier trial, Klein became doubtful of Krapp's guilt; having heard of voiceprints and their usefulness in other cases, he decided on a bold and unique move.

New Jersey law did not permit their introduction as evidence for the prosecution, but the statutes did not bar their use for the defense. This he pointed out to Judge B. Thomas Leahy, who was to preside over the trial, and he obtained the magistrate's consent in the hope that the technique might be of help to the accused. It was an unusual tactic, but Klein was a prosecutor who believed in the state's responsibility to see justice done — in this case to open the door to any evidence that might be helpful to the defendant.

Accordingly Dr. Kersta was directed to obtain comparative voice spectographs and to disclose his findings under oath. This he did and his testimony so impressed the court that the case against Krapp was dismissed.

What Dr. Kersta describes as his toughest case followed the crash of a Pacific Airlines F-27 turbo-jet in California with the loss of forty-four lives. The cause of the disaster was a mystery to Civil Aeronautics Board investigators, who finally turned to the voiceprints expert, believing that a solution might come through the garbled and unintelligible voice of the co-pilot, Ray E. Andrews, which had been taped by the control tower. The recording had been played and replayed in the hope that government experts might succeed in learning what had caused the crash. However, they were finally obliged to abandon their efforts.

Dr. Kersta accepted his assignment with skepticism, but he was eager to try. First he sought to eliminate the static and engine sounds that had made it impossible to comprehend a single word from the recording; this he finally succeeded in doing by using an electronic filter. Then after days of untiring effort he was able to catch a few sounds of a human voice though no actual words could be distinguished. How to bring intelligible words out of such sounds was the next problem.

After much thought he decided to experiment with a process that he never had used before: he would make a voiceprint of every vocal sound on the filtered tape in the hope of being able to recognize at least one or two words, for he had already learned that there is a general similarity in the prints of a specific sound despite some individual differences.

Proceeding along these lines, he spent days speaking into the tape recorder those sounds which he suspected each voiceprint might represent. This done, he voiceprinted his own utterance of that sound, spoken as a word, and compared the two prints, his own with that from the control tower tape. He hoped that there might be a noticeable similarity of words.

The first word he tried was "stick" but that was wrong. He tried again with "skit" and with "strip," but the tests were again negative. This he continued until he finally received a positive reaction — the word "skip." Encouraged, he experimented with "skipper," but there was still something lacking. "Skippers" was the word that finally coincided.

Further work of this kind went on for days until at last Kersta had made fully comprehensible the entire taped message recorded at the tower — "Skipper's shot . . . we've been shot . . . trying to keep . . . ."

That was all, but the denouement of the mystery came long afterward with the discovery of a discharged revolver in the wreckage of the plane. It had been registered by one of the passengers. The other details remain a secret hidden in the graves of the ill-fated travelers and crew.

Another of Dr. Kersta's extraordinary achievements was of a far different nature with serious international implications. Oddly, his involvement in this curious situation followed a telephone message from the editor of the *Daily Telegraph* in London. The editor referred to a published radiotelephone conversation purported to have taken place between Gamal Abdel Nasser, then president of the United Arab Republic, and King Hussein of Jordan during the brief Middle East War of June 1967.

Monitored by Israeli electronics experts, the dialogue, in Arabic, purportedly disclosed a secret plot connived by the two Arab leaders to blame the United States and Britain for aiding the Jewish state. A tape recording of the exchange became worldwide news when spokesmen for Israel summoned correspondents to hear the recordings in these words.

Nasser: Will we say the United States and England or just the United States?

Hussein: The United States and England.

Nasser: By God, I say that I will make an announcement and you will make an announcement, and we will see to it that the Syrians make an announcement that

American and British planes are taking part against us
from aircraft carriers.
  Hussein: Good, all right.
Within hours the story of the alleged conversation appeared
in major newspapers in many countries. The Arab leaders were
indignant, blaming Israel for what they called an outrageous
hoax. Even neutrals were skeptical, suggesting that the voices
of the Arab leaders could easily have been imitated.

Among the many doubtful ones was the editor of the London
Daily Telegraph — and he had an interesting idea. He had read
of voiceprints and of their inventor, Dr. Kersta. Could this
man, he asked himself, use his equipment and methods to
determine the veracity of the conversation? He decided to
inquire and made a transatlantic call to Kersta in New Jersey.

Kersta was interested of course, but he said that he would
do nothing without the consent of the State Department.
This was soon forthcoming, and a day later the American
scientist had before him a copy of the controversial tape and
an authentic recording of Nasser's voice obtained two years
before. How to compare them, in a language that Kersta did
not understand, presented a difficult but not insoluble
problem.

He began by replaying the Arabic tape and selecting twenty-
five different sounds that he knew were distinctly Arabic,
sounds like "ah" and "ee" which are common in that tongue
though there are no exactly similar sounds in English. Working
day and night, he produced voice spectrographs of the basic
sounds, comparing them with graphs of the voice definitely
known to be that of Nasser. The voice pictures matched perfectly, and Kersta announced that beyond doubt Nasser had
been one of the parties to the conversation. This conclusion
was verified by observers who understood the Arabic language.

Kersta was unable to obtain a tape of Hussein's voice alone,
but he assumed that if he could identify Nasser as one of the
speakers, it was logical to accept the other voice as that of the
Jordanian monarch. His final judgment was fully accepted even
by neutral skeptics, and another accomplishment was
recorded for the voiceprint technique.

Doubtlessly, no assignment undertaken by Kersta for use of
his voiceprint methods attracted as much media and public

attention than the one in which he was called on to authenticate the voice of Howard Hughes, the multimillionaire recluse, speaking from his home in the Bahamas to a panel of newsmen in Los Angeles.

The time was January 7, 1972 at the height of a bitter dispute in which the celebrated financier branded his biography written by Clifford Irving as an outright fake despite the author's vigorous assertion to the contrary. This, of course, was considerably before Irving admitted that his book was a fake.

The long distance telephone discussion had been requested by Hughes who for more than fifteen years had shunned the press, refusing to be interviewed on any subject.

From the Los Angeles end of the long distance telephone line, seven prominent members of the press hurled question after question at the man on the Caribbean Island. They covered a wide range of subjects but it soon had become obvious that Hughes' main purpose was to support his claim that the purported interview written by Irving was a hoax.

When the extraordinary interview finally ended, it became necessary to prove that the voice accepted by the interviewers as that of Hughes actually was his. The newsmen were positive that it was; Irving, on the other hand, insisted that the reporters had been speaking with an imitator. This he maintained in spite of the fact that Hughes had quick and correct answers to questions involving minute details concerning events in his earlier life — happenings of which he alone would have accurate knowledge and memory.

The controversy was at its height when Kersta was called on for an expert opinion. He had been contacted before the interview and had in his possession tapes of Hughes' voice taken years earlier testifying before a Senate sub-committee. Obviously, the long-distance interview had been adequately taped.

For days Kersta worked in his laboratory comparing spectographs of the two sets of tape. He was in no hurry to pass judgment, for he knew that his reputation was at stake. However, when he did announce his decision it was in a formal statement to the effect that beyond the slightest doubt the tapes matched — the voice recently heard over long distance telephone, he asserted, was definitely that of Howard Hughes.

Kersta, however, was eager at this point to substantiate his judgment. He called on Dr. Peter Ladefoget, a professor of phonetics at the University of California in Los Angeles. In early years Ladefoget had been publicly critical of Kersta's work with voiceprints; his opinion on the current issue now would be of great value, Kersta believed.

However, the Los Angeles scientist, after thorough study of the tapes, agreed with Kersta in his findings that the voice beyond doubt was that of Hughes.

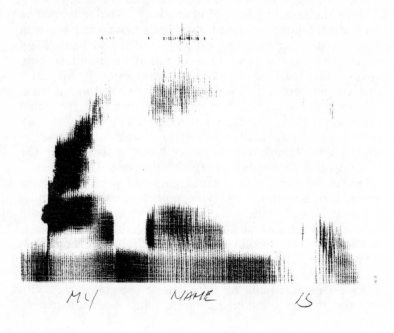

A voiceprint — a graphic pattern of the human voice

As retired head of the Voiceprints Laboratories in Somerville, Dr. Kersta looks forward to a wide expansion of his system in criminal identification as well as in industry and business. He hopes for the day when hundreds of thousands of voiceprints will be filed in central police headquarters just as fingerprints are kept and classified. In this way a suspect's voice spectrograph in a case of blackmail, extortion, or the like could be compared immediately with those of known offenders.

However, his plans extend still further. His system, he believes, can be effectively used to combat the increasing use of stolen credit cards, and it can be of still further value in determining quickly what is wrong with business machines. "Every machine makes a noise," says the inventor. "When it's working right it makes one kind, and when it's out of order it makes another kind — another use for the voiceprint spectograph."

So there is plenty of research ahead for Dr. Kersta. And when he is not busy, though that is seldom, he finds diversion in a few favorite hobbies such as gardening, philately — "and my wife."

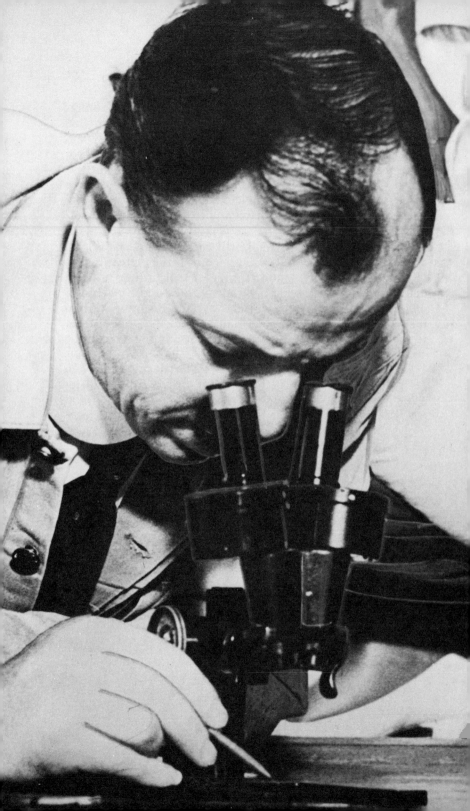

Chapter 17

Even a Snail Helps

MANY HUNDREDS OF YEARS AGO a Phoenician came upon an amazing wonder of nature while watching a snail moving slowly over the ground. His observation, centuries before the use of ultraviolet light in the crime laboratory, is described in a statement by Dr. A. J. Pacini, director of the Pacini Laboratories in Chicago.

He says that the detection of crime by the use of ultraviolet light is based on a discovery in the shell of a snail in the ancient city of Tyre. There, snails moving at their usual slow pace were found to secrete a whitish fluid which turned to a rich violet color when exposed to sunlight for a few hours. He relates that an enterprising Phoenician used this phenomenon to produce the first royal purple dye. The doctor further notes that the principle involved is the fluorescence of certain substances under exposure to ultraviolet light which, in the case of the snail, came from the sun.

The man who watched the snail ages ago of course would be amazed to learn that today ultraviolet light is one of the most valuable tools in the crime laboratory, enabling technicians to detect bloodstains that have been so thoroughly washed that they are invisible to the naked eye, or to disclose writings with invisible ink and the alteration of documents.

The development of the practical use of ultraviolet light as a weapon against criminals came very slowly, as did the use of fingerprints, hair, dirt, and other techniques of crime detection. In fact, a total of 106 years were to pass between the first scientific discovery of ultraviolet light radiation and its introduction into criminal investigative work.

Explained in lay terms, ultraviolet light is that part of ordinary light which in the spectrum lies beyond the visible violet. While invisible to the human eye, its rays cause certain

Edward O. Heinrich (see p. 186)

substances, such as blood, to glow — to fluoresce. Blood, for example, takes on a greenish color with a bluish tinge under ultraviolet light.

In the long and exciting history of scientific progress, credit for the discovery and basic understanding of ultraviolet light goes to Johann Wilhelm Ritter, a German physicist. The discovery occurred in 1801 during Ritter's intensive study of the effects of light on certain chemical substances. Ritter learned that ultraviolet wave lengths are longer than those of the x-ray and shorter than those of ordinary light.

Exactly 101 years later, on a warm August night in 1902, a tall, handsome man of thirty-four made his appearance in a Baltimore hall before the staid members of the American National Academy. Robert Williams Wood, a native of Concord, Massachusetts, and a graduate of Johns Hopkins University, had been invited to demonstrate to one of the most august bodies of scientists in the country what he had achieved in his intensive study of ultraviolet light.

Ignoring the stares of his doubting elders, Wood walked briskly to the rostrum with a pipe clenched in his teeth and a satchel in his hand. From his bag he removed an arc lamp enclosed in a lightproof iron box fitted with a small window that he said would not admit ordinary rays of light.

Skepticism turned to intense interest as the young speaker related the results of his experiments. To illustrate his words, he exhibited photographs of trees and mountains he had snapped through a new filter of his own design that permitted only the ultraviolet rays to reach the film. His pictures showed no shadows, though they had been taken in the sun.

Next, showing photographs of the moon taken through his specially designed filter, Wood pointed out that the dark and light areas were in far sharper contrast than in pictures taken in the conventional way. As the listeners slid forward in their chairs, eager to catch every word, the speaker set the rays of his lamp on certain minerals that he had brought with him and demonstrated how they fluoresced.

His lecture was reported in scientific journals, and physicists for months besieged him with questions, yet the young man from Johns Hopkins still did not realize that his work could be applied to crime detection — or, if he did surmise — he was not prepared at that time to stake his reputation on such a claim.

It was not until five years later that the next advance came about. A technician in the Vienna police department had been reading one of Wood's scientific papers, in which the author pointed out that if the writing on a legal paper had been tampered with erasures could be detected by the use of ultraviolet light, even if the alteration could not be revealed in any other way.

This gave the Viennese technician a new idea: he reasoned that forged checks and legal papers could be exposed by the same scientific process. Correspondence with Wood followed, and Wood suggested that invisible ink could be made legible in the same way.

Only two years passed before forgers, betrayed by ultraviolet light, were being sent to prison and spies were being unmasked.

How practical applications of Wood's technique were gradually turned to other types of crime investigation is related by David Loth in his book, *Crime Lab*. Among the many interesting cases he relates is one involving the finding of human bones in a California national park. Close by lay a weathered knapsack and a waterlogged book of traveler's checks.

Since the signatures on the checks had been obliterated and no worthwhile clues to the victim's identity were available, the investigators in desperation sent the checks to the FBI laboratory in Washington. There they were exposed to ultraviolet light, and the once illegible signatures soon became visible. The dead man was finally identified as a young conscientious objector from Arizona who, it was learned, was hiking to the home of his parents.

Luke May of Washington State, who, as stated earlier, gained a wide reputation as a criminologist, demonstrated the practicality of the "magic light," as some called it, in a number of important cases. Some of these he relates in his book, *Crime's Nemesis*, devoted to laboratory techinques. In one case the guilt of a murder suspect was established when an ultraviolet examination of the prisoner's hair proved it to be the same as strands found on a brush left behind at the scene of the crime. A pomade used by the suspected killer produced the same purplish fluorescence, and a baffling mystery was solved.

May, who specialized in forgeries, also used ultraviolet light in this branch of his criminalistic work. Once he was called on to study a disputed will that, to the naked eye, showed no writing variations; no erasures could be detected, even with the help of a microscope.

Before passing final judgment, however, May took the testament into his laboratory and studied it under the ultraviolet lamp. It did not take him long to discover that many parts of the will had been altered. Different inks used by a forger who evidently was well satisfied with his work glowed with a telltale violet color, revealing glaring forgery.

One of the most dramatic examples of the use of ultraviolet came in a puzzling murder mystery from the laboratory of Edward Heinrich in northern California, and as a result a brutal killer went to a federal penitentiary for the rest of his life, though he was once convinced that he had made his detection impossible.

His name was Jesse Watkins, a civilian employee at San Francisco's historic army base, the Presidio. He had worked for some years as an assistant to the base's veteran stablemaster, Henry Chambers, a favorite among both officers and enlisted men.

Watkins's service had ended abruptly with his discharge for laziness. A bitter argument followed, with Watkins threatening to kill his former employer. In self-defense Chambers had drawn his revolver and fired, inflicting only a superficial wound. In the desperate struggle that ensued, Watkins seized the weapon and beat Chambers unmercifully over the head until he fell senseless to the floor in a pool of blood. Watkins, fearing that he may have become a murderer, bound the bleeding man's legs and arms, gagged him, and left him to die.

Skulking over the fog-swept paths of the Presidio on the way to his room, Watkins realized his hazardous situation. His white shirt was stained with his victim's blood, as were his hands and face. Reaching his lodgings little more than a mile away, Watkins was met by two roommates who caught sight of his gory appearance and asked what had occurred. Watkins had a ready answer. "I was held up on my way home," he said, "and when I resisted one of them shot me right here," and he pointed to the gunshot wound inflicted by the stablemaster, explaining that it had bled profusely.

As soon as he was alone in his room his attention turned quickly to the shirt. To send it to a laundry would be dangerous, he told himself. His only recourse lay in washing out the bloodstains until not the faintest trace of them remained.

He filled his washbowl with cold water and with brush and soap scrubbed the garment vigorously. This he repeated with hot water and then again with cold. He spent fully two hours doing this until he was thoroughly satisfied that the spots had been completely washed out. He even spread the shirt over a table, examining it inch by inch under the glow of a strong reading lamp. The soaking garment was hung up to dry, and in the morning Watkins folded it carefully and put it in his bureau drawer.

In the meantime the murder had been discovered by soldiers who suspected something was wrong when they heard hungry horses neighing. Chambers, during his long years of service, had become known for his meticulous ways, which took him to his duties with the precise regularity of clockwork. Fearing that he might be ill, the servicemen forced their way into his room above the stables and found him dead.

With the murder thus revealed, army police and city detectives joined in an intense investigation. They found the lethal gun and sent it to the laboratory to be examined for fingerprints. There were no other clues. As days of inquiry passed, one of the detectives was told that a man named Watkins who had been discharged by Chambers had been overheard remarking that the man deserved the kind of death he had suffered.

Watkins was located some time later and denied any knowledge of the crime. Because he appeared to be too eager in asserting his innocence, the investigators undertook a thorough search of his room and insisted on seeing the garments he was wearing at the time of the murder.

Satisfied that the well-scrubbed shirt could not possibly betray him, Watkins took it from his bureau drawer and handed it to the officers together with other clothing. There was further questioning, and in the end one of the detectives told him that he would take all the clothing including the shirt to headquarters. Watkins laughed. "How will they ever help you to solve the murder?" he asked with a show of sarcasm.

When laboratory examination of the clothing failed to produce a clue, the investigators finally agreed that they had reached a deadend, and after further discussion they decided to summon Heinrich as a last resort. He arrived at headquarters hours later and listened to an account of what had occurred. He was handed the suspect's shirt with an explanation that it had been thoroughly examined and showed no bloodstains.

"Don't be too sure of that," Heinrich retorted, "though I admit it does appear to be perfectly clean."

"Just what do you mean by that?" he was asked.

He then explained the use of ultraviolet light and how it could reveal evidence of blood despite an apparently spotless appearance.

"Never heard of that," one of the officers remarked, trying to conceal his skepticism.

Heinrich took the shirt and Watkins's other clothing to his laboratory in Berkeley and set to work. He had often said that it took a full day to thoroughly examine any garment.

His scrutiny of the underwear and trousers was to no avail. Finally he turned to the shirt, stretching it over a table to be studied under the rays of the ultraviolet lamp. He had not gone far when he detected signs of radiation; portions of the linen began to fluoresce, showing a green and somewhat bluish light. Before long it became definitely apparent that the shirt was covered with bloodstains, which could not be seen with the naked eye but became visible under ultraviolet because the blood had penetrated into the linen fibres and could not be thoroughly removed by washing.

Heinrich's report quickly led to Watkins' arrest. He was informed of the expert's disclosures and a confession was demanded. For a time he parried every question, but hours afterward his hands began to shake and he showed other signs of weakening.

"All right," he finally blurted out, "I'll come clean. I killed him." And he related every detail of the crime.

The ultraviolet light examination and its results naturally became a dominant part of the prosecution's case, backed by the confession. Watkins was found guilty of murder and sentenced to serve the balance of his life behind bars.

Chapter 18

What Is the Answer?

THE ASTONISHING ACHIEVEMENTS of the crime laboratory confront criminologists and sociologists with baffling questions.

If scientific tools and techniques can make a single hair talk and produce effective clues from tiny wood chips and other matter, why are crimes of violence so widespread and increasingly brutal and daring? Why do not at least some criminals change their ways in fear of capture?

Why do not modern means of quick transportation and lightning-fast communication deter those who flaunt the law? Is it that the criminal mind does not fear arrest because of a strange certainty that the "perfect crime" can be conceived and executed? Or is it at least partly because lenient judges and opportunities for parole make the risk worthwhile?

There are many answers, and they go deeply into our present system of criminal justice and today's complacency about lawlessness. Many believe that our society sanctions too much consideration for offenders — their legal rights, long appeals, and too easy a life within the walls of our penitentiaries and reformatories. Others contend that our penal institutions have become "crime schools," preparing inmates for greater violence for profit, and that our current methods of rehabilitation have failed.

And there are those who argue that insufficient attention is being given to crime prevention and to juvenile delinquency in its earliest stages; that we are content to kill the mosquitos while failing to drain the swamps in which they breed.

No doubt all these factors play contributing parts, though today increasing attention is being given at the federal, state, and local levels to abort criminal tendencies at the starting point.

The end of the trail . . . .

Society itself also comes in for sharp criticism. Too many intelligent men and women are too busy to meet the responsibilities of American citizenship and loath to "waste" their time in jury service. Witnesses to crimes are too often reluctant to come forward to aid the authorities lest they become involved, with a consequent loss of time. And some are fearful of retaliation from criminal elements.

One of many interesting comments comes from Dr. Harry Moore, chairman of the education of justice department of the University of California at San Jose. Contending that there is no relation between the laboratory and the crime rate, he declares that only about 2 percent of crimes investigated by technicians actually produce worthwhile physical evidence, a view contrary to general public opinion and to the views of others in crime detection. Moore laments the fact that in some jurisdictions crime laboratories are poorly equipped and the technicians not adequately trained. The results are, he says, that under these circumstances law enforcement agents cannot effectively interpret scientific findings. He fears that some criminals are more cognizant of these conditions than those fighting to enforce the law.

A somewhat different approach comes from Dr. John I. Thornton, assistant professor of criminalistics at the University of California at Berkeley. Dr. Thornton emphasizes that when police laboratories are overtaxed by work of lesser importance, time is taken from crimes of far more serious concern, such as homicides and other cases involving violence. Objectives, he points out, must be reappraised.

While recognized authorities announce with a degree of pride that there has been some drop in America's crime rate, no one will dispute the fact that it is still far too high with serious violence menacing the safety of men and women especially in our large cities. The bandit who once snatched a woman's purse and ran now beats or shoots her so that he cannot be identified in case of arrest.

Late in 1972 Attorney General Richard G. Kleindienst announced that serious crime rose only 1 percent in the first six months of that year — the smallest increase for any comparable period in the past twelve years. At the same time he stated that seventy-two major cities reported reductions in crime for the first half of the year.

These comparisons were made with previous six months figures issued by the FBI, statistics showing that in the first six months of 1971 violent crime increased by 11 percent and property crimes rose 6 percent, compared to a 1 percent increase in both categories during the greater part of 1972. Such a change he credited to the "efficient and devoted work of police chiefs and peace officers" throughout the nation.

While this does offer some degree of encouragement, let us view the attorney general's statements in the light of the staggering cost of law enforcement. A study by the Law Enforcement Assistance Administration reveals that nearly $8.6 billion were spent on all forms of law enforcement and criminal justice in the United States during the twelve-month period ending July 1, 1970. The same survey disclosed that three-fourths of the total expenditures, approximately $5 billion, were spent to support police activities. These figures doubtlessly have increased materially in later months.

Few will question the amazing expense involved, but many will pause to wonder what these billions — or perhaps some of them — would accomplish if spent on slum clearance, poverty and hunger relief, education, and other necessary social advances. But the war on crime must go on regardless of cost. It must go on and it must be won.

How can we do it, many ask. There are no simple answers. I do not pose as either a criminologist or a sociologist. But some elements of the problem challenge the thinking of all of us in the great lay population. First, let us acknowledge that our "great American society" is sick — very sick.

One of its many symptoms lies in the decadence of the home. What part does the home play in everyday life today? Economic conditions, in many cases, compel both parents to be bread-winners. Little if any time is left for home life and parental guidance. As the late Julian Alco, a widely known penologist and warden of San Quentin Prison once said, "We are born in the hospital, married in a hotel, and buried from the under-taker's. What role does the home play in our lives?"

If home life is declining, what substitutes do we provide for our children? Playgrounds, organized recreation, handicraft programs — are they adequate? How much attention is being given to the need for harnessing the gang spirit of boyhood and turning it into constructive, lawful effort? This is one major phase of crime and delinquency prevention. The church and synagogue command attention. Too many dedicated clergymen preach to half-empty pews. What example do we parents set for our boys and girls?

And there is the whole staggering problem of criminal justice. Are our prisons too greatly concerned with punitive rather than with rehabilitative effort? Recidivism remains shockingly high throughout the nation, even in California, recognized as probably the most advanced state in penology, with its steadily increasing number of psychiatric programs aimed at studying the criminal mind in order to understand its failings.

Then there is another issue, already referred to in this chapter — public indifference toward law enforcement. Too many of our citizens cry out for stricter obedience to traffic laws, only to run to politicians when they find themselves with a traffic tag. For some, violating the law has become something of a game.

Those who wear a badge, risking their lives day and night for the protection of the community, too often suffer from the derision of the citizenry. They have lost the respect to which they are entitled.

Ramsey Clark, former United States Attorney General, in his book, *Crime in America*, writes sharply of society's responsibilities. He insists that crime reflects more than the character of offenders. Rather, it discloses the character of society. He blames society, then, for the useless lives of criminals.

The answer, if we accept Clark's views, is that society itself is largely if not wholly to blame. What are we, the members of today's society, going to do about it?

Index